SURVIVING DIVORCE
A new beginning

Warren Gregory

Publisher:
Warren Gregory

www.survivingdivorce.com.au

Contact the author:
warren@survivingdivorce.com.au

Copyright © Warren Gregory, 2022
All rights reserved. No part of this book may be reproduced in any form or by an electronic or mechanical means, including informational storage and retrieval systems, without permission in writing from the author, except by review.

First printed: May 2022

ISBN: 978-0-6454993-0-8

Printed with:	IngramSpark, Australia
Editor:	Ruth McIntosh
Cover and layout:	Ivan Smith
Cover Photo:	Stock photos Dreamstime

The author acknowledges Aboriginal and Torres Strait Islanders as the traditional custodians and Australia's first people. Their culture, identity and connection to country are respected and honoured.

*Dedicated to those
men, women and children
who suffer in silence through divorce.
Who cry out for an understanding ear.*

FOREWORD

I look back on my time of being a pastor in six churches over 30 years with a great deal of warmth and a deep sense of honour, all mixed with sadness. From the beginning of my training at Bible college I had a deep compassion for people in general and for what is known as the *ecclesia* – the gathering, the church. Coupled with that however, I struggled with the institution, which confusingly, is also known as the *church*.

It was also while at Bible college, that I had the life-changing opportunity to do post-graduate studies in Christian Counselling. This exposure to the field of psychology shaped my understanding of the Scriptures, and in turn my theology shaped my psychology.

The warmth I experienced from the church came from the relationships I built, and from the honour I received from those who opened their hearts and lives to me in my counselling office.

It was in my pastor/counsellor role that I met Warren and Jenny and their family. They were a warm and engaging young couple. They clearly loved their children, were staunch advocates of the sacredness of family and a model of a healthy couple deeply involved in the local church. Warren was busy with a growing business and other commitments within our congregation. Jenny interacted with other young mums despite the busyness of schooling, the toddler years and the demands of home.

And then, to the surprise of all, the 'wheels fell off' as they say. Church attendance decreased, leadership roles finished, Warren attended Sunday worship from time to time on his own or with the children, and eventually a broken man sat in my office, lonely, confused, and bewildered. My memory of his opening words at our first session were, 'I don't know what's happening ... something has changed, but I don't know what it is ... what have I done? ... what does Jenny want?'

This story, the experiences of this little family, is part of why I struggle with the church, the institution. How have we missed the mark as a people-group who base the whole purpose of being upon the ideology of love, forgiveness, and grace, and yet families hurt and no one knows? Instead, the mechanics of the institution – Sunday worship, board meetings, Bible study groups, multiple 'family-centred' programs – take precedence, priority, energy and resources, leaving little for families in crisis. Added to that, how much do church demands contribute to the crisis? Busyness is the antithesis of a quality, family life.

To read *Surviving Divorce: A New Beginning* is to enter the inner struggles of an ordinary family. If this is your story, you will be able to relate to much of what Warren says, and may also be equipped for the journey that lies ahead. If this is not your story, the insights you read here will do much to give you a deeper understanding of the hurts and struggles that lie waiting at the door of a broken marriage and a broken home, and yet the possibility of a new beginning.

Martin Gillespie
Counsellor & Social Worker (Family Violence)

INDEX

ix   Introduction

1   It Wasn't Supposed To End This Way

11   So What Do I Do Now?

17   Run And Hide Or Face And Confront

33   Asset Distribution

39   Custody Of Your Children

49   Learning And Recovering

55   Communicating With Your Ex-Spouse

63   Finances

73   Communicating With Your Children

81   Through The Eyes Of Children

91   Single Again And Loving It

99   New Relationship

INTRODUCTION

I wasn't expecting a life-changing encounter that day as I walked into the foyer of one of my clients. We were meeting to discuss the next building project I was to design and manage for them. After working together for seven years, this would be just another site meeting – or so I thought.

I was 34 and in the middle of a complicated separation from my wife. This meeting would be a wonderful distraction from the all-consuming emotional roller coaster that is divorce.

I indulged in a small joke with the receptionist.

'June,' I said, 'never go through a divorce!'[1]

June shot back, 'Well, actually I am!'

June was in the process of filing for divorce – at the very time when I too was working through similar issues. June's response to my throw-away line set me on a life-changing journey of discovery and ministry. Tears welled as she briefly shared the story which led to separation from her husband.

'Why was this so life changing?' I hear you ask. 'After all, people separate and divorce all the time.'

Stay with me.

I did not know June's husband – in fact I knew very little about her family situation. A few weeks went by after our encounter. It was a Sunday and I was in church – about 75 kms from June's workplace. At the end of the service a friend asked if I would meet a man, Peter who was going through a situation similar to mine. Peter was also recently separated from his wife and doing it tough. I was more than happy to meet him. Perhaps I might be able to help him or, better still, he might help me.

---

1. All the incidents mentioned in this book are true, but (apart from a few exceptions which are acknowledged) no real names are used.

Peter didn't look familiar, but just before I got to him God told me Peter was June's husband. 'Yeh right,' I thought. As we were introduced I asked if his wife's name was June. He looked bewildered.

'How do you know that?'

I'm not sure who was more shocked – Peter or me. We shared our very similar stories there and then. It was immediately obvious that we understood what the other was talking about, the emotions we were feeling, the sadness that too often became all-consuming and overwhelming. A supportive friendship was birthed that day, and cemented over weeks and months. We were able to unload to one another, providing rare but valuable mutual encouragement. My relationship with June remained unchanged; she had her own support network. Sadly, their marriage dissolved but, years later they both remarried and are moving on with their lives.

Meanwhile, I was still trying to make sense of my own situation. God brought similar friendships into my life – 'chance' meetings with guys in the same situation. I came to realise that God was using me to minister to them, and they were encouraging and supporting me in return.

Eighteen years have gone by since that meeting with Peter. Eighteen years of working through all the issues divorce brings. Working to understand, make sense of, deal with, and even escape the deep pain and suffering. How thankful I am to be in a place where my experiences can assist others in the recovery process.

You may be reading this book for a range of reasons. Perhaps you are in a struggling marriage. Perhaps your marriage has already dissolved and you are looking for answers – any answers, which will help make sense of your situation. Perhaps you are looking for the 'so that's what happened' understanding we are all looking for – and a clear road to recovery and freedom. Perhaps even ideally hoping for a fulfilling and successful re-marriage.

When I found myself suddenly labelled as a 'divorced man', I certainly went on the hunt for answers and a road map to recovery. I was part of a church family, so that was the obvious place to start. That didn't go so well. Sadly, the church at that time – or at least the church family I was involved in – didn't know how to handle divorcees. I got the picture pretty quickly. Whether churched or un-churched, people are just people. Some are a great help – others are certainly not!

Introduction

I saw some churches provide a 'ministry' to those going through divorce – a place where divorcees can meet to share their experiences and gain coping strategies. I found that the leaders, who were often from seemingly wonderful marriages, had little understanding of the emotional dynamics involved in going through marriage separation. No matter how hard they tried to understand and help, many attendees just didn't feel understood or helped.

Some attendees were so emotionally absorbed in their own situation they didn't want to – or perhaps couldn't – open up in that environment. What is needed is an environment where pain and emotion can safely spill into the room. An environment which is safe. And believe me when I say 'spill', I mean spill. I have never seen such intense emotion poured out. Despite my experiences, God's people can play an important part in the recovery of His people from broken relationships.

How did I navigate this part of my life? I tried one-on-one meetings with other guys, I saw my counsellor and I read books on marriage separation. God used a wonderful Christian counsellor/pastor to assist my recovery from a broken marriage. My experience was that God put the right person in the right place for the right stage of my recovery process. I was seeing Martin (his real name!) when I could see the writing on the wall, before the period of separation. He was alongside before, through and after my broken marriage.

I used to think that 'real men' don't need counsellors or psychologists. I now know that 'smart men' use counsellors and psychologists in the same way they use a mechanic for their prized Holden SS Commodore or Softail Harley Davidson. Do you get your car serviced? Of course you do! How about giving yourself the same treatment. Go and get a 'service'. You might be surprised how well you run afterwards. I was surprised when a pastor friend of mine who I greatly respect casually said, 'I must go see my psychologist next week to process some stuff'. What surprised me was not that he was seeing a psychologist, but that this was HIS psychologist.

So why did I write this book? Primarily because I could not find one book on marriage separation which was written from a Christian perspective by someone who had actually gone through divorce themselves! The authors were either counsellors or psychologists who seemed to write about grief counselling. I got tired of reading what stage

I should be up to by now and how I was 'supposed' to behave for the benefit of all involved.

Some people suggested that I 'just get over it and move on with my life.' I just wanted to swear at them ... or worse! Don't tell me just to get over it! If only it were that simple. One client actually said, 'Well, you're off the hook. Just get over it and move on.' I didn't spend much time around that person.

Primarily I wrote this book for guys! We guys are hesitant to be open with one another, especially when it involves airing our failures and inadequacies. Openness and vulnerability – especially in a group setting? 'Are you kidding me! You want me to tell you what happened in front of all these guys I don't even know?' Yes, I know you don't have any failures or inadequacies, but most of us other blokes do!

Sure, I can keep meeting with you guys one on one – and I'll keep on doing that as the Lord leads – but I've chosen to write my experiences down, with the prayer that this helps more guys – and girls – progress further in their recovery from divorce.

I have called this book *Surviving Divorce*, because at the early stage of a divorce that is all you are interested in doing. Honestly, in my experience, right then, that is all you can do. My prayer is that this book will help you to realise that ...

... not only can you survive divorce, you can thrive through and after divorce.

A couple of things to be aware of as you work your way through this book. While all the stories I share are real, all of the names associated with those stories are fictional to protect people's privacy. This book is unashamedly part biography. It is based on my experience as a husband, father and man, so the language and focus are predominantly that of a husband, father and man – but there is subject matter relevant to both men and women. Please be assured, there is no intention whatsoever in this book to apportion blame or negative connotations to anyone involved in my journey.

Introduction

My sincere thanks go to Ruth McIntosh (Editor) for turning my rambling and poor grammar into free flowing text. A final product that does justice to the serious topic that is divorce recovery.

Surviving Divorce – A New Beginning

ONE

It Wasn't Supposed To End This Way

It was about 9pm. I stood beside the limousine I had hired for the big occasion, waiting for Jenny to finish work and walk out of the building. She saw me there, all dressed up (unusual for me) with a big smile on my face. Her workmates quickly guessed what was going on.

It was a very special evening. We were chauffeur-driven to the top of the Dandenongs (a mountain range close to Melbourne, Australia), picking up a pizza on the way. I had planned it all – bottle of wine, pizza, me dressed up as if I was going to a ball, a casual cruise up to the top of the Dandenongs in a limousine. We stopped and looked at the beautiful lights of the city below while the stars danced approval above us. It doesn't get any more romantic than this (well, it was the full extent of my romantic capabilities).

We had been dating for four years. Jenny was only 15 on our first date and I was 18. I had already gained the approval of her parents, as every noble young man did. We were two kids very much in love and with not a care in the world. I realised some weeks later that I didn't even ask Jenny to marry me that evening. Marriage just seemed the natural next step for both of us and we began planning the big day.

Jenny came from a fine family with loving parents. Her father was a leader in the church, her mother a good homemaker and a strong Christian foundation was established. Jenny was quite a sort too. What else can I say? All the necessary boxes were ticked. She was the one for me. I must have ticked most of her boxes too. Getting her parents' approval was less painful than I expected.

My family included mum and dad (love them to bits), two older brothers and a younger sister. We were brought up in the church and our families had many similarities. In fact, both families were very good friends. We'd known one another for many years.

Jenny and I met at church, spent time together in youth group and knew each other quite well before we started going out. We were both very sporty. We would go to each other's basketball matches to watch and cheer. I would spend most of the time after my game getting her to tell me how good I was (I know, I know), and after her game complimenting her that she played well.

We shared a keen interest in music. I played the trumpet, Jenny the saxophone. Playing in the church band was a great way to share our love of music and at times we would play duets at functions.

Surely marrying a beautiful young woman with similar values, interests, likes and beliefs would be the foundation for a fantastic marriage relationship. We dotted all the i's and crossed all the t's when it came to the dos and don'ts of courting.

We were married nine months after that romantic evening. I had our life all planned out – although we had to borrow money to get back from our honeymoon. We would have a fantastic marriage and beautiful children who would grow up to love the Lord. I would provide for my family and love my wife.

After three months in rental accommodation, we moved in with my parents. We were both studying and wanted to save money. That was not a good move. My parents weren't difficult to live with, but newlyweds need their own space – sometimes lots of it. It wasn't that I wanted to frolic around the house naked, but living with the folks was a serious disadvantage.

I left university and got a job as a draftsperson, and Jenny got a job as a medical secretary. We built a house some distance from our parents and were finally on our own. I was fulfilling my God-given role of providing for my wife.

We planted a new church in a town on the outskirts of Melbourne with four other couples. We were paying off our new home, establishing a new local church and our relationship was going great guns. We had planned a family after about four years of marriage, but Jenny was ready after two.

Things were going well with work and we had the house, so why not? Our first child, Leo, was born. What a fantastic blessing he was and is. I will never forget his birth and thinking, *how can anyone not believe in God if they have seen a child born.* I remember thinking *life can't get any better than this!*

Over the course of the next four years we had two more children – two beautiful girls, Makayla and Brooke (I am biased, but they are truly princesses). I started a building design business in partnership with another Christian man. Things went very well and we grew to 13 staff in two years. To be honest, I get tired of people using a business as the reason for marriage failure. This may be true in some instances, but it is not a general rule and was certainly not a key factor in the failure of my marriage.

God did however have a serious lesson for me to learn at this time. I was in the lounge room reading Ecclesiastes – you know, 'everything is meaningless' and all that. It was about 9pm and the kids were in bed. My business partner called. I was surprised to hear from him at this time of the night.

'What's up,' I asked.

Nonchalantly he replied, 'I'm just standing outside our office watching it go up in flames.'

'WHAT! What do you mean our office is going up in flames?'

The dry-cleaning business next door to our office was on fire he said, and there were fire trucks and people everywhere.

'I'll be there as fast as I can!'

'You don't need to come down.'

'Of course I'm coming down! You tell me our office is on fire and I don't need to come down. What is the go with that?'

I told Jenny what had happened and jumped in the car. It was only 15 minutes from home to the office. As I turned off the highway to head through a quiet part of Beaconsfield, I saw the flashing lights of a police car. I drove past two policemen standing beside a body lying on the road under a blanket. I remember the surreal setting – calm, peaceful, dark. *Wow, this is bizarre,* I remember thinking. Then the Holy Spirit reminded me of Ecclesiastes – 'Everything is meaningless'.

I drove on. As it turned out, everything was fine, apart from the dry cleaners which was destroyed, but I returned home with a new perspective on work, God, life and family.

I never heard anything more about that body in the news or in conversations around town, but God used that glimpse to tell me something I needed to hear. My identity and security did not lie in my achievements as a businessman nor in how successful I was in people's eyes.

'What has this got to do with divorce?' I hear you ask.

We can't simply isolate one life event, however significant, from other lessons God has taught us. Our life is an unfolding story. Every event adds a piece to the life puzzle. It contributes to the overall picture. Being able to recover through divorce requires an understanding of things that have happened in your past.

Life continued to get better and better – or more successful. Our church congregation grew to about 200 in seven years, and Jenny and I had important and rewarding roles there. I was a regular worship leader, Bible study leader and occasional preacher (the thought of that scares me even now.) Jenny was running the playgroup and had a good response from the local community with a number of mums attending who were non-churched. Our kids were still very young and enjoyed the church family, as did we. They were enrolled in the local private Christian school.

The business became more and more profitable. We were becoming very well recognised in the industry with at least four of our clients being in the top ten major domestic builders in Victoria. Our commercial clientele was also expanding. I was able to indulge in every young man's dream – a Holden SS Commodore. Come on, you know you all want one! I purchased a Holden Jackaroo for Jenny.

I was 32, we had almost paid off our home and put a deposit on a block of land in Pakenham – on the highest hill in the most expensive estate I could find with 270 degree views – from Port Phillip Bay to Mount Baw Baw. I was going to design the most fantastic home for my beautiful wife and three fantastic kids. Nothing was too good for them.

I didn't think there was anything wrong or ungodly about our chosen path in life, but just because it was our chosen path doesn't mean it is God's chosen path for us (hhhmmm, have to ponder that one). We appeared to have it all. We were the 'perfect Christian couple'. The sad part was that,

It Wasn't Supposed To End This Way

while things on the outside looked picture-perfect, the same could not be said about the inside.

What happened next came as a shock to us all – and I mean all – to me, Jenny, our children, my wider family, our friends, everyone who knew us.

We planned a summer holiday in Noosa, Queensland. My brother and his wife had moved to Queensland, but sadly had separated. In November 2002 Jenny said she wanted to go and stay with my brother's ex-wife in Queensland for three days before we began our long-awaited Noosa holiday. She said she simply wanted to bring closure to the separation of my brother and his ex-wife – to get things right in her mind. Jenny would fly up with our two girls: Makayla (4) and Brooke (1). I would drive up with Leo (6) and we would have our family holiday as planned. I had such a good time with Leo driving to Queensland from Victoria. We stayed overnight at a motel. It was a bit of a blokey adventure in the four-wheel drive Jackaroo. Don't go there guys! Yes, it was all bitumen driving.

Leo and I arrived on Bribie Island to meet Jenny and the girls. The moment I got out of the car it was obvious something was not right. Jenny seemed very unsettled – she seemed to simply want to go and do her own thing. I found her state of mind very unsettling. Our communication had suddenly become blocked and I had no idea of how to connect with her. Looking back now I wonder if we ever really connected in the first place. That holiday became a nightmare. Our life of comfort, security and a positive future was in total disarray. What had changed? What had happened?

By the end of that holiday, Jenny was adamant that we had to move to Queensland. The life that we were used to in Melbourne was not what she wanted anymore. During our two weeks in Queensland I remember sitting in the motel on the phone with my business partner in total confusion saying, 'I'm moving to Queensland.'

I had no idea what to do and spent most of the time on the phone in tears trying to make sense of it all. After that trip, I think I went into a phase of denial. Jenny seemed incredibly unsettled and, within a week of coming home, simply returned to Queensland to stay with my ex-sister-in-law for an unspecified period of time. She took two-year old Brooke and was gone for two months. I found that period of time very difficult.

When Jenny returned, she was still wanting to move to Queensland. Subconsciously I felt that my marriage was under serious threat, but all I could think of was what to do in this situation. What do I need to do at my end to keep our marriage alive. If that meant moving to Queensland, then that's what we would do, although I hated the thought of moving to a place where we knew very few people.

It meant leaving the business, finding a new school for the kids, a new house, a new church. Man, I was in total confusion!

I was also in a state of denial. *Everything will be OK, we will move. Jenny will be happy and we will start all over again. We are a good Christian couple and divorce is not an option.* This is what I kept telling myself.

Jenny appeared confused about life and what she now wanted from it. What had caused this? Where did I go wrong? WHAT HAD HAPPENED!!

I remember sitting down and asking Jenny – as if my life depended on it, 'Are you sure you want to move to Queensland!?'

Her answer was a defiant, 'Yes!'

Maybe a fresh start in a new environment would allow us to reconnect. I thought, moving seemed the only way to save the marriage.

I do remember sitting in the recliner late one night. The lights were off and everyone else was in bed. I said – or more accurately told the Lord, 'Lord, if you don't want us to move to Queensland, you'd better stop us because that's exactly what I am planning to do!'

Over the next few months, we made regular trips to Queensland to look for a place to live. I took interviews for work, we looked at schools, etc., etc. – all the things you do when relocating your whole life to another state. I made arrangements to split the business partnership. It was all happening. Things were starting to fall into place and, as much as it didn't sit right with me, moving interstate was becoming a reality.

About six months into the relocation process I realised that all hard work was beginning to fall on me. Jenny had become more and more distant from me and the kids, from the move to Queensland and our life in general. I asked her again, 'Do you still want to move to Queensland?'

'No, not really,' she replied.

I was filled with sheer relief and great thankfulness to God. It had seemed a foregone conclusion. However, my relief was short-lived. I soon realised that this may mean the end of our marriage, but I was still in denial. I refused to admit this – marriage is for life. We would sort this out and Jenny would wake up from the dream I thought she was in.

We were advised to get counseling to understand what was happening and re-build our marriage. Unfortunately, we never did make it to any counselling sessions.

For about six months, things were a mess. Life was simply indescribable. We were living in the same house, but love, commitment, passion and joy was replaced by resentment, selfishness, loneliness and heartbreak. We were a married couple living under one roof living separate lives.

Jenny suggested I should move out on a number of occasions. I refused. There was no way I would leave my wife or my three children. I had no reason to and didn't want to. I was also sure that God didn't want me to.

I have spoken to many men who sadly have lived or are living through the same thing. I am very strong about doing what is right in God's eyes. For me, and for many other men, it is right to stay in the home and continue to seek marriage reconciliation. I do acknowledge though that this may not be the best advice in all situations.

You will hear me state many times throughout this book, '**Every situation is different**'. People are often not prepared to take responsibility for their choices or be accountable for their decisions. It breaks my heart when Godly, caring men tell me they left their home, wife and children because their wife said, 'I've had enough' or 'I don't love you anymore' or 'We can't keep going on like this' and just wanted them out. The flip side is men who simply wanted out because they couldn't live in such an environment or work through the issues.

If you are in the situation I am describing, and it is still a safe environment for you to be, can I encourage you to hang in there, with the guidance and help of trusted friends or a trained Christian counsellor. There is no guarantee your marriage will recover, but it's a 'stay and work' attitude rather than a 'run and hide' attitude.

In the end Jenny said that if I wouldn't leave, she would. By this time, I had set up my office at home so that I could be more flexible. After three to four months Jenny left. I was still thinking that she wouldn't go because we were a Christian couple.

Jenny left in September 2004. I will never forget that day as long as I live. We sat down with the kids in the lounge and, rightly or wrongly – I am still not sure which – I asked Jenny to explain to the kids why she was leaving. There was undoubtedly an element of resentment in my insistence. I wanted the kids to know that this was Jenny's decision, not mine.

I was in tears – and I'm teary describing it to you. Three-year-old Brooke came over and put her arm around me, as she still reminds me to this day. What a terrible, terrible thing for three young children to go through.

Which is better for children, an explanation of a parent's departure as it is happening, with both parents present, or being told after the event? I will let the psychologists argue that one out. All I know is, decisions are often made in circumstances of unspeakable turmoil and that God is sovereign over all circumstances.

I have given you a brief rundown of our marriage. I suspect that it is similar to the experiences of many other couples, whether they are followers of Jesus or not. As you read my story, I wonder how much of it is yours. There may be circumstances you can definitely relate to – others which are miles from your own experience. Whichever is the case, as I speak to men and women in broken relationships or marriages, one thing remains consistent: it is painful and at times devastating to the point of considering suicide.

According to the Australian Bureau of Statistics there were 113,815 marriages in Australia in 2019 and 49,116 divorces granted. Interestingly, the divorce rate has been decreasing over the years. This coincides with a decrease in the rate of marriages by a staggering 31.9% from 2019 to the first six months of 2020. I used to think that divorce was not an option for Christians, but you cannot and should not try to control decisions or the behaviour of others.

I have painted a marvellous picture of my marriage, but it broke down, sadly to the point of no return. This proves to me that, no matter how strong a relationship looks on the outside, only the people involved know what it is really like. The truth is, the day we returned from our honeymoon, I thought we may have made a terrible mistake. That may be a story for another time, but I was a Christian man who had committed himself to his wife. Divorce was not an option so we would make the most of what we had. I am thankful that we had many happy years together and brought three wonderful children into the world.

While this book is about divorce recovery, I still believe that divorce is not God's plan nor God's desire for His people. Matthew 19:6 says, 'So they are no longer two but one flesh. What therefore God has joined together, let not man separate.' Every effort should be made to salvage your marriage. Many people I talk to who have gone through a divorce, men and woman, agree that ...

It is easier to work on a marriage than it is to work on a divorce.

Discussion Starters

- We usually start off with the best intentions for our marriage.
- What is seen on the outside is not always what is going on on the inside.
- Emotions can cloud the reality of your situation.
- God wants what is best for our marriages.
- It is easier to work on a marriage than it is to work on a divorce.

TWO

So What Do I Do Now?

Well, it had actually happened. Jenny left to live with her parents 40 minutes' drive away. The following few days were a blur. The life I had known for nine years was gone.

I do however, distinctly remember asking this question immediately after Jenny left the house.

'What on earth do I do now?!'

My emotional state was shock, surprise, disbelief. I was not in a place to be able to process what had just happened. I could not even think of what to do next. Simple survival activities were all I could think of. Just the mundane things of life ... going into the kitchen for a glass of water; walking from one part of the house to the other to see how the kids were doing; getting a cup out of the cupboard for Brooke who was thirsty.

Leo said, 'I'm hungry'.

I just looked at him. *How am I going to feed them? I don't cook!* Simple everyday activities suddenly became massive chores. I was there physically, doing whatever I could manage, but I was not really there mentally – but the fact was I still had to look after our children who didn't understand the gravity of the situation.

It really was a case of just focusing on how I was going to get through the next five minutes ... then the next five minutes ... and the next. I couldn't think too far ahead of that. I was trying not to let my mind run away with all the possibilities of what might be. I was fortunate to have the distraction of needing to care for our children. I was not used to living my life half an hour at a time, but that is exactly what was needed in the early stage after Jenny left.

Within that first hour, I remember contacting the most trusted and safest person in my life to tell them what had just happened. I process by talking, so talking to my trusted friend helped me to function. I had to learn very quickly to accept the help of others.

So, how do you deal with the 'What do I do now' question in the first hour of the separation?

... *stop and deal with what is immediately in front of you.*

As time progresses, you become more able to cope with the practical realities of your situation. This is when you will have opportunities to stop, rest and begin to process your thoughts and questions.

When you leave the family home, or your spouse leaves, a million questions run through your head. The questions will be vastly different depending on your life circumstances and your personality. Your questions will depend on variables such as: status of relationships, ownership of the house you've been living in; the type of job you have – if any; children – if any.

Here's a snapshot of some of the questions I remember asking myself and God – in no particular order:

- What's going to happen with the kids?
- How am I going to work and look after the kids?
- What are the people in the church going to think of me?
- Am I going to have to sell our house?
- Do I need to take the kids out of school?
- How much money am I going to have to pay Jenny?

- What are her family going to think?
- How are my clients going to react?
- What's going to happen when I meet her boyfriend?
- What if her boyfriend hurts my girls?
- What if my kids don't want to stay with me?
- How are the kids going to play their sports now?
- What sort of future are the kids going to have?
- Who will pay off the cars?
- How could I be so stupid as to marry Jenny?
- Why did I not see this coming?
- I can never lead in church again!
- I don't have anyone to live the rest of my life with now!
- What if I never find someone who will love me again?

So many thoughts race through your head when the reality of your situation hits home. Each person's experience and thought processes are different, but there are sure to be a myriad of questions and realisations. Many of these will be thrown up by your understandable panic and confusion. Nevertheless, many will require decisions to be made at some stage – and knowing that is scary.

In addition to the many questions you will be faced with, many thoughts seem to take control of your mind.

'How do I stop and think through stuff when I have so much to sort out?!'

'How will we survive? He isn't giving me any financial support.'

'I have to find a job, and how can I do that when I still have to look after the kids?'

'She won't let me see the kids and now she's living in the house I paid for – with her boyfriend!!"

Yep, all these situations occur – and many even more complex ones.

That is exactly why we need to stop and work through these thoughts in a calm and controlled manner.

I was given this very helpful advice

> ... *never make a big decision when you are in an emotional state.*

Decisions made when in an emotionally unstable place are often the wrong decisions.

If you are a list person, as soon as you are able, sit down and write down a comprehensive list of the issues which face you. It may be wise to involve trusted others in this process as you may not be able to think very clearly.

Then begin to put these issues in priority order – *your* order of priority. Why have I emphasised 'your'? Many well-meaning but ill-informed people are sure to tell you what you should do in many different situations.

Other men may say, 'Mate this is what I did and you should do the same thing ... mate.'

Remember, they are not you, they don't know the complexities of your situation and they don't have the same priorities. You are one of a kind and your situation, while similar to other people's, is unique. At the end of the day, you, your wife/ex-wife, and any children will have to live with the decisions you make.

Seek advice in areas you feel you need guidance, from professionals or well-trusted friends. And ...

> ... *be aware that some people will tell you what you want to hear rather than what you need to hear.*

So What Do I Do Now?

A harsh word spoken by a true friend can save you a whole lot of heartache down the track. This pains me to say, but don't assume that Christians always have better advice than those who don't know the Lord.

I decided to find a good family law solicitor, just in case I needed their services for child custody issues. My first port of call was a secular firm in the city. I met with a lady recommended by a friend, but left feeling unsure that she would go in 'to bat' for me and the kids.

My second option was a well-known and respected Christian law firm. That visit left me feeling it would all be a waste of time to contest child custody. Their attitude seemed to be 'get what you can, and be happy with that' – a very defeatist attitude. Thanks mate!

My third option was a family lawyer recommended by a very close friend. I felt he really knew his stuff and that the kids and I would get a fair outcome. As it turned out, I did need his services and was pleased with the results he achieved.

I discovered very early on that one of the most intimidating weapons family law solicitors wield is the threat of time limits. Letters would always come with a time limit condition, accompanied by a threat of further action. My advice is, don't be intimidated or rushed into action because you are given a time limit. Your lawyer will let you know if time is an issue with any request. Spend the time you need to make the most informed decision based on truth, not on fear and intimidation.

Before this upheaval, you may have had a good idea of where your life was heading. Now that will need serious re-evaluation. Take time to think through what is best for you, your spouse/ex-spouse and your children, then begin to work towards those goals. Keep in mind that you can only control your decisions and your choices. You can't control the decisions or choices of your spouse/ex-spouse.

One thing that took me a long time to come to terms with was the fact that, in the eyes of most other people, the breakdown of our marriage had nothing to do with fairness or taking responsibility for actions. They saw it as a private matter between two people. They didn't care why or how it happened. The sooner you accept that fairness or justification for decisions is irrelevant, the easier and less painful moving forward will be. Remember that your idea of fair may be completely different from that of your spouse, friends and family.

I have discovered that moving forward successfully, even when children are not involved, always requires communication and a willingness to 'suck it up' – the readiness to accept difficult situations even when you think you are being dealt with unjustly. The thing which keeps me focused is remembering that it is all about the best outcome for our children. To put it bluntly, basically my wants and wishes don't matter much anymore. Sounds harsh I know! After all, aren't we constantly told, 'You're the most important person in the world?' I'm afraid that, for the good of our children, ourselves and those close to us, we're not!

Discussion Starters

- Deal with your immediate circumstances.
- Stop, rest and evaluate.
- Identify the known issues and potential issues.
- Prioritise the issues.
- Plan and work towards positive outcomes for everyone (including your spouse).
- Be wise about whose advice you accept.
- 'Suck it up' and don't be selfish. It's not all about you, however justifiable such thinking may seem.

THREE

Run And Hide Or Face And Confront

Having the kids with me at the outset was a real blessing. They were a welcome distraction from the amazing loss I was feeling. My attention was drawn away from my pain as I focused on them and tried to help them deal with their world – which had so abruptly turned upside down. It was incredibly difficult to juggle my own emotions and to be there for the kids. I now believe that God was providing everything I needed at that time with a perfect measure of His intervention and strength, while allowing me to learn the lessons He wanted me to learn. He enabled me to grow through this experience and He continues to help me grow day in day out, but I am so much more aware of His help now.

Just in case you're thinking that I coped wonderfully with the separation, don't be deceived. The first time the children were in Jenny's care, I spent two days in bed unable to sleep, eat or even think. I still struggle with knowing what to call Jenny. Is she my ex-wife, first wife, or old spouse? Old spouse sounds terrible, doesn't it?

I had the wonderful care of my parents at this time. They were an incredible support. I spent most of the time either in tears or curled up in a ball wanting the unrelenting knot in my stomach to disappear, or both. I am so blessed that my coping mechanism is tears. Tears provide a wonderful emotional release that is harmless to the body – except for the exhaustion they can cause. I know a number of men who cannot release tears in such circumstances and resort to much more harmful coping mechanisms.

I also learnt that God has set a perfect example of fatherhood for situations like this. It is so hard to see our children suffer pain and experience failure. We desperately want to take it from them and bear the pain ourselves – or we want to ensure they succeed in whatever they attempt. Indeed, we want to protect our children from pain. It should hurt us when they suffer pain or experience failure. But rather than taking the pain from them we need to get alongside them and support them through it. The Bible tells us that this is what God does. *The Lord is near to the brokenhearted and saves the crushed in spirit* (Psalm 34:18).

Here is the thing – we are actually doing our kids great damage if we stop them from experiencing pain or make sure they don't fail. I have come to understand that God wants what is best for me in His perfect will and, if that means allowing me to suffer pain and failure to take me to the next step, then bring it on.

Sure, God could have taken all the pain of the marriage breakup away. He could have stepped in and allowed everything to fall into place for my, Jenny's and our kids' complete recovery, but would I have learnt why things turned out the way they have? I came to realise that we had married each other to fulfil our own needs and not the needs of each other.

Have I learnt everything I could in relation to this divorce? Of course not, but I understand that I will learn what God wants me to learn and I just have to let the other stuff go. Would I have understood the impact our decisions had on other people? Would I have gone into another marriage and made the same mistakes? Would I want to help other people by sharing my experience? One of the things I love about the Lord is His ability to discipline us, teach us and love us in the same 'breath'.

It is time to tell you about two early morning experiences. Near the beginning of our first week in Queensland on holiday (see Chapter 1), God woke me at 3.30am. As I lay there, God gave me a vision of a decaying body floating immediately above me. It was totally clear – as if it was actually there. I could see the flesh hanging off and the bones exposed. The vision lasted for about two seconds and then it was gone.

About five days later I experienced what I now call 'The Nightmare'. I was beginning to realise that my life was starting to fall apart. One night, again at 3.30am, I was suddenly wide awake in what I now like to call 'the zone', knowing that something supernatural was about to happen. I knew

God had woken me up to show me something. I lay there for at least half an hour, waiting for God to speak or to do whatever He was planning to do. This type of experience was very new to me at the time. Eventually, God said, 'I want you to let Jenny go.' I knew that God was asking me to respond physically, not simply to make a decision. How did I know it was God? I just knew. This was definitely not something I wanted to do.

I found myself holding my hands up in the air. I was lying on my back on top of the sheets, with Jenny beside me. I can still see myself with my fists clenched as if holding onto something, then opening my fists as if releasing a captive butterfly. I symbolically let go of my wife and offered her up to God. I let Jenny go as God had asked me to do. I lay there for some time, tears in my eyes, as I came to grips with what had just happened. Even though I had acted out this release physically, letting Jenny go emotionally took a very long time.

About 5.30 or 6am Jenny woke up and saw me lying there, obviously engaged in a spiritual battle. I was silent and still, but my face told her that something was going on. I was still 'in the zone', but quite aware of what was going on around me. Then God told me to tell Jenny to get our daughter Brooke (about two at the time). She asked why and I simply said that I needed her to get Brooke. I was still unsure about the full meaning of what was happening. Jenny brought Brooke in.

I held Brooke's hand and God said, 'Let Brooke go.'

I was very hesitant. I didn't want to let my daughter go. God asked me to do this a number of times. Eventually I obeyed and let go of Brooke's hand as if setting her loose. Then God asked me to do the same thing with Makayla and Leo. Jenny was very confused about what was happening and I was worried about frightening the children.

'No God,' I said.

It would have been about 6.30am by this time and I was exhausted from the whole ordeal. Even now my whole body tenses as I recall these experiences, and I become physically and emotionally drained but, believe it or not, that morning I actually went back to sleep. We had planned a trip to Brisbane that day, but my spiritual experience wasn't over. God had much more to show me.

I was still in bed when God spoke again, 'I want you to spend the day with me.'

I argued with him, telling him that we had planned to go to Brisbane – as if He didn't already know.

God simply said again, 'I want you to spend the day with me.'

I love the way God leaves the choice up to us, but He can be very persistent. Eventually I agreed and told the family I couldn't go with them. After they left, I somehow knew that God hadn't planned a fun day – it was going to be a hard slog. I lay in bed until 10am, trying to avoid the inevitable. Eventually I got out of bed and asked God what He wanted. I grabbed a Bible. Guess where God took me? That's right – Ecclesiastes!!

During the next two to three hours God revealed who I was and what I was like. Before you jump to any conclusions, let me clarify. In the world's eyes I was well respected, by Christians and non-Christians alike. This however doesn't count for much in God's eyes. I would read, see some truths, cry, then read, have God show me some more truths about myself, then cry some more and so on.

Man, I was seriously disciplined by the most magnificent father a son could have. After two to three hours of discipline, rebuke and conviction I had read all of Ecclesiastes. I was broken.

Then God very matter of factly said, 'Right. Now let's read Proverbs.'

The next two to three hours were amazing. Before beginning to read Proverbs I was probably about as low as I had ever been in my life. I was emotionally and physically drained of all self-worth and achievement. I had nothing left to offer. I had been disciplined! Now, God began the process of re-building His 'temple' in my humbled human body.

As we worked through the book of Proverbs God started to reveal truth in ways I had never thought possible. I began to get a glimpse of what the Bible means in Romans 12:2 when it says, 'be transformed by the renewal of your mind'. God was loving me, His child, for whom He sent Jesus, His own Son, to earth to die on a cross. As we read through Proverbs, again I read and cried – but these were tears of joy and revelation, not tears of sadness and pain. God revealed, I cried, read more, cried and was filled with gratitude, love and hope.

Our perfect Father was now loving me and re-building my hope – showing me that true hope is only found in Him. He was giving me instructions for life. He even told me not to associate with a particular person anymore, because of their influence in my life – a church leader

I had known for some time. It was an amazing day – one which I still remember as an incredible day of revelation and an example of how to love your children through discipline, guidance, grace and compassion. How good is our God!

Please don't misunderstand. Because God revealed all this to me, doesn't mean I now have everything on track and am super-spiritual. Nothing could be further from the truth! The more I know, the more I realise how much I don't know. My reliance on God becomes more necessary every day.

I am so thankful that God chose to love me through discipline, revelation, guidance and grace.

Here we were, three children and a man who was more comfortable in the corporate world than the home. I was a single parent raising three children while running a business. Despite all the confusion and turmoil, we managed to agree on childcare arrangements quite early on. I had the children Thursday to Sunday night and Jenny had them Sunday night to Wednesday night (child custody issues are discussed in chapter 5). This seemed the fairest arrangement and allowed the kids to see both of us. It was also very important to disrupt the kid's routine as little as possible. Our whole life continued to revolve around our hometown of Pakenham.

Given my new circumstances, I had to make a number of very important decisions which involved a wide range of emotions, including:

- Embarrassment
- Guilt
- Resentment
- Anger
- Fear
- Loneliness
- Bitterness
- Jealousy

- Frustration
- Helplessness
- Failure
- Determination
- Compassion
- Forgiveness

If you are going through or have been through a marriage separation, I'm sure you can relate to some or all of these emotions. I had to learn to give myself the freedom to experience the full range of emotions and let them run their course. As you read through that list – and perhaps even add some of your own – you will notice that some would be seen as negative emotions, such as loneliness or anger. I came to realise that the emotion itself is not negative. It's how we react to that emotion – or allow that emotion to shape our decisions – that can have negative, even destructive results. If you want to recover from a marriage breakdown, responding appropriately to your emotions plays a vital role in the process.

For us Aussie blokes, emotions are easily suppressed or drowned with a couple of beers or a quick adrenalin hit from a visit to the car races, or even the thrill and challenge of a good poker tournament. The reality is that, when that fix is over, the ignored emotion comes knocking even more loudly on your door, demanding your attention. This is where the real battle is. I found myself confronted with a very important decision

… do I acknowledge and confront or do I run and escape?

As I talk to men at different stages of the marriage breakdown journey, I often see the destruction caused by refusing to confront problems, or allowing emotions to manifest in destructive ways.

About a year after Jenny left, I felt I was to attend a meeting held by an organisation which assists men in my situation. You may have heard of such groups or even been to their meetings. They do a wonderful job helping men deal with marriage separation issues. My experience was somewhat different. I wasn't really sure why I needed to go, but trusted God's prompting. Once again I had ignored His call – this time for about three months. You know – the whole *I don't need to go because I don't have anything to offer them anyway,* or *the them, me* thing was going on in my proud head.

There were about six men at the meeting and it was 'chaired' by a chap I'll call Damian. I'd read an article about Damian and the group in the local paper. That's what caught my attention and led to God's prompt.

It was confronting showing up to a strange place where I didn't know anyone, to talk about the most emotional event that had occurred in their life and mine. I 'bit the bullet' and went anyway. I'd had a quick chat with Damian a few days before to find out how the meetings were run. I parked the car, walked across the carpark and into the foyer and was met by Damian who directed me to the meeting room. About seven guys were sitting around a table. It felt a bit like attending a board meeting – a setting I felt at home in. The way they interacted made it obvious that I was the 'new guy'. They looked at me curiously. Some even seemed excited to see me.

The meeting started, apparently as it usually did, with a minute's silence. There was an empty chair at the table. We were told that the chair represented the one in five men who took their life as a result of marriage breakdown. That minute of silence was reflective and sombre as we thought of the plight of many men (and undoubtedly women) involved in marriage breakdowns.

After this ceremony, those present were invited to share with the group. A small figurine placed in the middle of the table could be claimed by anyone who wanted to share. This meant that they had the floor and no-one could interrupt until the figurine was placed back in the middle of the table. It was 'up for grabs' as it were.

Being the new kid on the block, I felt all eyes were on me, anticipating what I might say. The pressure was intense. I had told myself before I went to the meeting that I was just going to observe and lie low. Being a rather determined bloke, I was not going to give in to the unspoken expectation. For what seemed like five minutes, but was probably only 10-20 seconds, silence filled the room. At last Damian grabbed the figurine and began sharing his story. It was sad.

Damian's wife took off with another chap, taking his young kids with them. He had never seen or heard from them again. Wow, I felt so sad for Damian, who would have been in his late thirties or early forties. What I very clearly heard in his voice was the resentment he felt towards his ex-wife. I could certainly understand how that might dominate his thought processes. The rest of the guys had obviously heard Damian's story before. The figurine was placed back in the centre of the table and silence again filled the room. The pressure on me intensified, but I stood firm to my decision to observe.

Another chap, Andrew, took possession of the figurine and began to share his story. He told another horrific story which involved custody battles, intervention orders and even the threat of murder. Andrew calmly explained to the group that he was so upset about the judge not giving him what he deemed to be fair custody of his children that he had threatened to kill his wife. This threat – the result of his emotional state at the time – led to an intervention order being placed on him. He had not seen his children since.

In no way do I sit in judgement on these men and the ways in which they have reacted to the circumstances they found themselves in as a result of their own actions and the actions of others. I can fully understand how such situations arouse a myriad of emotions. Yet again I emphasise

... it is the actions resulting from these emotions which shape our future.

It was surprising to hear chuckles of understanding when Andrew said he told his wife he was going to kill her. The chuckles said, 'Yeh, we get it brother!'

Currently in Australia, close to sixty woman a year are killed by a current or former partner. This does not account for the physical, sexual, emotional or mental abuse occurring in Australian homes on a daily basis.

It is no wonder many women are living in fear. It is so important these recovery gatherings don't contribute to the possibility of such abuse.

The figurine went back on the table and once again silence set in. It became obvious that they were not going to let me get away without sharing my story.

I grabbed the figurine and all the men seemed to sit up in their seats with anticipation. I felt my journey was far less 'dramatic' than the ones they'd shared, but when I began talking about the children and the custody battle I was in, the meeting took a whole new turn.

At that time, Jenny and I were involved in mediation to renegotiate custody of the children. Mediation had failed and the matter was currently in the hands of solicitors to finalise the agreement. Before attending this meeting, I had been at peace with the process, however painful and expensive it was, and expected that the outcome would go as planned and that equal custody would be approved.

I explained to the group that the solicitors were dealing with the situation, and it would all be worked out and approved. Well, the authority of the figurine took a dive. I starting being peppered with questions left, right and centre. It was quite bizarre.

Damian was most concerned that I had nothing in place to stop Jenny from 'taking off' with the kids as she was in another relationship. Andrew and some of the others told me how much they had spent on solicitors' fees. Their costs ranged from $8,000 to $40,000 plus. Make no mistake, their intentions may have been good. They wanted to save me all the heartache and pain they had experienced. I realised that this was the purpose of these meetings. To protect other men from making the same mistakes they had made.

What did I learn from this meeting and why did God send me there? I now believe that it was to show me the damaging impact of decisions based on giving in to negative emotions. When the meeting concluded we all grabbed a cuppa, went outside and continued more casual, less guarded conversations. I got talking to Damian. Our chat confirmed my suspicions that he was 'anti-woman' and 'anti-solicitors'. This had understandably resulted from his life experiences. Damian's motivation for helping other men was admirable, but:

It is not wise to lay our emotional baggage on others.

I do believe it is helpful to encourage men to talk about their experiences.

While I left that meeting in a concerned and slightly fearful state, once I recognised where a lot of the comments were coming from and what was driving them, I was able to properly process the discussion. However, with some of what I'd heard this took a number of days. Remember also that I had already had some 12 months of professional counselling before attending this meeting.

Another very important part of the recovery process is allowing yourself to grieve. Grief is experienced whenever there is loss. We all understand that loss is experienced in many situations – after a death, expected or unexpected, even after loss of security. It is important to remember that divorce involves huge loss – the loss of a relationship and, in many circumstances, loss of security for both partners. Experiencing the emotions we have been discussing is part of that grieving process. The grieving process takes time and must be lived through. Once that is done, life can again become rewarding and fulfilling.

At times we can become stuck, unable to move onto the next step, or we can try to avoid one of the steps and move to the next. We can often move backwards and forwards between emotions. Remember, there is no predictable or absolute pattern.

What are the likely steps?

- Denial
- Anger
- Acceptance
- Repentance
- Forgiveness

It may be helpful to recognise which emotion you are predominantly feeling at any time. Allow yourself the time to process the emotions you are feeling. It was suggested to me that I start writing down my thoughts in a journal. As I reflected on my journal entries, I saw that in the early days of separation my actions were often driven by my emotions. It was encouraging to see how over time, my actions became more and more driven by thoughtful evaluation and long-term perspectives.

I got sick and tired of hearing people say, 'you're not in this alone'. Even though I hated hearing it, it was true. Humbling myself to the point of allowing someone I trusted into my journey to give me support was incredibly important. There are times when an important decision needs to be made and you may not be in the correct frame of mind to make a good call on that decision. You may decide to ask the advice of one or a number of people – it's your call.

Life can be very complicated at the best of times, but I eventually realised that my life consisted of three important areas:

- Mind
- Body
- Spirit

Don't panic! I am not going to get all freaky on you, but let me tell you why I mention these three distinct areas. I found that they all need to be attended to and maintained. If you do not have a spiritual belief, just deal with the first two. However, my viewpoint is that the first two cannot operate to their best capacity without considering the role of the spirit.

Mind

What we believe to be true, what facts we base our decisions on, how we order our life and our understanding of different circumstances are all primarily challenges of our mind. I was able to talk with a professional counsellor, not so that he could tell me what to do, but to help me understand why I thought the way I did and why I had made certain decisions.

For example, I could not understand why my wife had left me. I believed I had fulfilled my role as a husband by providing for her and loving her to the best of my ability. What had gone wrong? Our discussions about this question helped me re-visit my understanding of why I married Jenny in the first place. What were my – and her – expectations of the marriage?

As I explored these questions, I came to a better understanding of the possible reasons for the marriage break up and my role in that – whether or not I wanted to admit and accept it. The past could not be changed, but I was able to develop a greater understanding of what drove my thought processes at that time. Was my mind driven by truth or pre-conceived ideas? Where did the pre-conceived ideas come from?

I could also discuss questions like, 'What is the best outcome for my children now?' and 'How are the children likely to respond in certain situations?' Discussions with trained counsellors and wise friends, and reading professional literature gave information and guidance about various situations, and helped me to make more informed decisions about my children's future welfare.

I learned the importance of self-talk which can shape your future in negative or positive ways. Self-talk is inevitable. We tell ourselves things, not necessarily verbally, but sub-consciously, and we begin to believe them. These things can either be based on truth or be simply fictitious.

My spiritual life played a very important role in this area. Would I allow the Holy Spirit/God to show me the truth or falsehood of my self-talk? Would I ask for God's help to identify the lies of Satan? It is important to know whether or not your self-talk is true. When I detect a lie, I like to picture writing this thought on a piece of paper and, physically or figuratively, I throw it in the bin and leave it there – or better still burn it so it can't be retrieved. If I deem my self-talk to be true, I need to act on it, either by myself or under the direction and guidance of others.

An example of self-talk might be, 'What I said to him was OK because of what he did.' Is that self-talk the truth or a lie? The action that results from the answer to that question will impact other people and your own recovery. I am making it sound very important – because it is. The actions that result from self-talk can be extremely helpful or have disastrous effects – as Andrew from the men's group discussion found out (story told earlier in this chapter).

One of my biggest self-talk hurdles was *everyone will think I'm a failure!* This thought particularly applied to the church where I was well known and respected. It took a long time to overcome this lie. It would raise its ugly head just when I thought I finally had it licked.

If you want a wonderful reference on the battles of the mind, then I recommend reading *The Battlefield of the Mind*, a book by Joyce Meyer.

Body

Stress can have a very negative effect on our bodies, even if we don't use alcohol, drugs and the like. This hit home when my body decided to give way. After the trip to Queensland, I was under significant stress. Over the next 12 months, I wasn't eating properly and didn't exercise at all. My focus was on survival and I forgot to look after my physical well-being. However, the mind impacts the body. If I had understood what stress was doing to my body, I may have been able to avoid physical breakdown.

I was a naturally fit guy, able to eat whatever I wanted and not suffer the consequences, but I was unaware of what was going on inside my body. I had always had back problems but, because I managed it properly, my back didn't give me any trouble. About two months after Jenny left, I was in the shower, dry retching with the stress of the situation. Suddenly I heard something pop in my back and went down like a sack of potatoes. The pain was excruciating. I managed to drag myself to my mobile phone and ring my parents.

I couldn't think clearly, so they rang an ambulance. I waited in agony, trying not to move. I rang my best mate Aiden who is a paramedic. He was great and helped me through till the ambulance arrived and I was whisked off to hospital. The drugs they gave me for the pain worked a treat, but I was in 'la la land' for quite a while. Apparently, they call it 'truth serum' because, while under the influence of the drug, people tend to blurt out closely-held secrets. Who cares! It took the pain away. The doctors diagnosed a bulging disk. One of the first questions all the doctors asked me was, 'Have you been under any stress lately?' Yeh!!!

I spent the next two to three months unable to sit or walk fast or drive. I worked standing at my computer and managed as well as I could with the kids, with much appreciated help from family and friends. Doing it on my own just wasn't an option – and, believe me, eating humble pie is not something I enjoy!

Let's face it, one of the last things you're thinking about when your whole life has been turned upside down is, *Now what should I have for dinner that is nutritious? What will keep my body in tip top shape?!* These matters were certainly not high on my list of priorities, but I know guys who use physical exercise as therapy when under stress. Everyone reacts differently and you must do what works for you. Just try to keep it positive and productive.

I learnt to eat properly and get some sort of exercise as often as I could. I even learnt to eat well when I just wasn't hungry. My mind may not have needed the food – although I would debate that – but my body certainly did!

Spirit

Ah yes, the uncomfortable 'spirit' topic. Well, no matter what you think about God, Jesus or the Holy Spirit, my recovery would not have occurred without my awareness of a Heavenly Father who was constantly reminding me of His presence, love, grace and provision. I have already shared some of the spiritual journey and could share so much more. For me it was – and is – simply understanding that I do not have the strength to overcome many of the hurdles I encounter.

It is imperative to have professionals, friends and family as part of your recovery team, but they can't be with you 24/7 – and you don't want them with you 24/7! Often you are on your own. You may think that you're the only one who knows what really goes on in your head, but guess what, God does too. The Bible says He knows you better than you know yourself and has already provided a way for you to recover. You just have to seek Him to find it.

That's the great news! You can just ask and wait. Remember those two days I spent in bed inconsolable, while the children were with Jenny for the first time? God brought me through and out of that. 'Why didn't He just save me from all that pain?' you might ask. I've definitely asked that question more times than I can count. I hadn't actually sworn at God before all this happened and would be horrified if someone said they had. But, what I love so much about God is His desire for me to be real with Him. He can take it. I talked before about becoming aware of truths and discerning lies – well that is the job of the Holy Spirit. For someone brought up in the church, to all of a sudden become face to face with the presence and reality of God was a wonderful revelation.

So how was my spirit nurtured? It involved a lot of alone time with God, asking and listening for direction, discussions with wise Christian friends and family, and listening to worship music (*Sons of Korah* were wonderfully used by God – it's worth checking them out). It also included reading the Bible – often not liking what God was showing me – and other times just revelling in His amazing love and grace.

If you want complete recovery, involve God!

If you want a great reference on learning about God I suggest reading the Bible (ESV, New King James, Good News, to name just a few translations). God often took me to the place in the Bible which was relevant for me at the time. If you're new to this whole 'God' thing, I suggest starting with the gospel of Luke in the New Testament. Luke writes about the story of Jesus who I believe is the only way to God.

Discussion Starters

- Release your emotions in a safe environment.
- Allow your emotions to run their course.
- Remember, your journey is different from everyone else's.
- Choose to recover.
- Choose to learn and grow personally.
- Take care of your mind.
- Take care of your body.
- Take care of your spirit.
- Cut yourself some slack and get to know Jesus!

FOUR

Asset Distribution

In my conversations, particularly with men, I discovered that possessions often became a key issue during the divorce process. This was also the case for me. I had worked very hard for many years to build up our assets. It felt unjust that I could lose all I had worked so hard to build through 'no fault of my own' – that's what I told myself anyway.

If you have flicked straight to this chapter, I would suggest that your assets are very important to you. This is not a criticism, but it may very well determine how painful – and expensive – the asset distribution process will be for you and your ex-spouse. Am I suggesting that you should just let it all go for a smooth divorce experience? Not at all. I am suggesting that it is important to keep everything in perspective.

Going through the stop, rest and evaluate process outlined in the previous chapter may help you keep a healthy perspective on asset distribution. I often had to stop, recall my main priority in a particular situation and then act accordingly. Before our separation, when preparing to move to Queensland, Jenny and I put a lot of our possessions in storage. After the separation – although we hadn't itemised everything – Jenny went to the storage container to retrieve the items we had agreed she would have. I had a favourite office leather sofa which was now Jenny's. That sofa, only worth about $600, had an emotional place in my heart.

'Seriously!' I hear you say. 'A sofa held an emotional place in your heart?'

Remember, your emotions are heighted during such times and what is normally not important can suddenly seem essential. In addition, we were having difficulty sorting out custody arrangements – but, I really wanted that sofa! Then I asked myself, *Am I willing to jeopardise access to my children* to get *a sofa*? The answer was obvious. *NO!* Mind you, I still miss that sofa.

The possible asset outcomes after a divorce are vast and various. I had well-meaning people say, 'Get what you can as quickly as you can before it all gets nasty.' Others would say, 'Don't worry about any of your things. It is only stuff. You can always re-build.'

Neither of these is my advice, rather:

> *…think of the long-term implications for you, your ex-spouse and, most importantly, your children if you have any.*

A colleague of mine shared quite openly and emotionally about a broken relationship that had occurred about 20 years before. His deep emotions and brokenness were still very evident. This man had the means to easily acquire more assets, certainly now and probably even earlier in his career. When the relationship broke down, he simply handed the house, the car and everything else to his partner and her new companion, and left. Either he put no value on possessions or made a very rash decision at a highly emotional time, which is understandable. The depth of his raw emotions 20 years later, suggest it was the latter. I am glad that he is now happily married, living a very comfortable life, serving the Lord.

Another man's grief and pain were so deep that he couldn't bear the thought of seeing his wife again. He simply asked her to get what she wanted from the house while he stayed away, leaving him whatever she didn't want. He was left with very little. This man's subsequent financial struggle made it very difficult for him to rebuild his life and recover from the divorce.

Asset Distribution

I suggest that neither of these situations was handled very well. Both, I believe were the result of making major decisions while suffering deep emotional distress. This is understandable, but not desirable. It surely would have been better to have sought wise advice. The reality however is that some of these situations must be dealt with reasonably quickly; the luxury of time to process and evaluate may not be available. If you find yourself in a time-strapped situation, sit down with a wise and trusted friend (or two) who can listen to your concerns and desires – which will probably be all over the place. Your friends will be much less distracted by emotion and should be able to help you decide what you really want, prioritise your requests and, if need be, act on your behalf. Remember the sooner you accept help from others, the easier your recovery will be.

I have also seen situations where the fight is on for every last dollar and only equal shares are deemed to be the 'fair' approach. Whatever the situation, there are no hard and fast rules about asset distribution. Unfortunately, many cases are finally resolved through solicitors or, worse still, the courts.

The level of resolution is often directly related to the level of amicability and kindness shown during the marriage breakup. The more hostile the breakup, the more hostile the asset distribution discussions tend to be. You would always hope that an acceptable outcome for both parties could be achieved without involving solicitors or the courts or, worse still, children. Unfortunately, this is not always possible.

If you are finding distribution of assets becoming a real issue, your first port of call may need to be mediation. This can be arranged through organisations such as Relationships Australia. Keep in mind that both parties must agree to the mediation process for it to have any chance of working. Once again, it is important to have an open mind and keep communication as amicable as possible. For more information contact Relationships Australia and seek advice.

I found it a lot easier to see asset distribution as a business transaction. This helped keep emotions out of the way and led to a quicker and less painful resolution. The fact that Jenny had decided to live with her parents gave us time to evaluate our joint possessions because we were both living in acceptable furnished accommodation. When the time came for separation of the minor assets, we agreed to write down our wish list independent of one another, then we came together to compare our lists. We reached agreement, signed each other's list and organised a time for the transition to take place.

Even though we had agreed on who would have these minor possessions, it was a very awkward and tense moment when the time came for Jenny to take her share. She was helped by her sister, while I continued to work in my make-shift office in the lounge room, standing up because of the bulging disc in my back. I must confess that being put out of action by my back was handy. I didn't have to offer to help with the shifting. The situation was awkward enough as it was.

If you are the one collecting the possessions from your previous place of residence, I suggest you take a trusted and non-confrontational friend with you. I would avoid another family member if at all possible. The less emotionally-connected people involved the better. I remember assisting a friend who was collecting things from his house. This awkward situation was made easier because I had no relationship with the other party. People are funny creatures. We seem to be better behaved when dealing with someone we don't know and who doesn't know us. I'm not sure how that works. Perhaps we just want to give a good impression. If you know a friend may cause trouble, don't take him or her. The other possibility is to have someone else do the collecting for you. As I said before, there are no 'rules' in these situations. You need to make the best decision for the situation you find yourself in.

Just some things to consider:

- It is not worth sweating over the 'small' stuff.
- Your possessions are often only stuff and can be replaced.
- You have both worked hard for all the possessions you have.
- Have the long term goal in mind (for example, a small sacrifice now can lead to better communication down the track).
- Set a good example for your children. If you leave your spouse with as little as possible, the children may resent you for it later.

The principles which apply to the smaller assets, also apply to the larger ones such as your home, car/s, caravan, boats, etc. etc. Deciding who gets what share of the larger assets can get very messy. It need not be that way. Keep in mind this one simple philosophy,

...the more you dig your heels in, the more likely it is that you will be paying good money to your solicitor.

The degree to which you dig your heels in is your call and you will be responsible for the outcome – not the person giving you advice on which way to go. Be very careful about whose advice you listen to.

Just in case you want to know, our divorce resulted in a more or less 50/50 split.

Discussion Starters

- Beware of making decisions when emotion is strong.
- Treat asset distribution as a business transaction.
- Don't involve confrontationally-minded people.
- Don't sweat the small stuff.
- Have the long-term relationship in mind.

Surviving Divorce – A New Beginning

FIVE

Custody Of Your Children

One of the sad realities of marriage breakup is its impact on the innocent parties, the children. When we decide to marry, we and our partner bear the bulk of the responsibility for the success or failure of our marriage. The children, in so many ways, are just 'along for the ride'. I have shared in an earlier chapter some of the specific circumstances of my marriage breakup and its impact on our children. They will tell you about it from their perspective later in the book.

You will be able to find many statistics which suggest it is better for children if they are young during a divorce and an equal number of statistics suggesting that it is better if they are older. I have had endless discussions, even arguments, about the advantages of divorcing when children are young. Many argue that, because younger children don't understand all the ins and outs of the messy situation, they adjust to a new lifestyle sooner rather than later. Others argue that it is better when children are older because they can process information and circumstances better, and ask the right questions.

I am not going to give an opinion either way. Suffice to say that neither situation is beneficial for children. In saying this, I am not referring to situations where children are being psychologically or physically harmed while living under an abusive marriage. I have not had any experience of this situation and do not pretend to have the wisdom, understanding or knowledge to speak into such a scenario. People close to me certainly have.

As I have already said, Jenny and I have three children: a son, Leo, and two daughters, Makayla and Brooke. At the time of the separation Leo was 7, Makayla was 5 and Brooke was 2. They were all very young. They are now 25, 23 and 21 respectively. They speak of some of the ways the separation has impacted them in Chapter 10. I had no intention of asking them to do this, but I was delighted when Brooke suggested that it might be helpful for my readers to gain an understanding of how my divorce impacted them. Who knows, it may even cause some of you to rethink the predicament you are in and turn your marriage around. I give more detail about how I see the impact the divorce had on my children in Chapter 9.

This chapter will focus on custody issues. I've learnt that one of the first questions to surface in most discussions about divorce is, 'Are there children involved?' If the answer is, 'Yes', then 'How many and how old are they?' That is certainly something I ask early on when discussing a potential divorce with a husband, wife or couple.

The marriage of a close friend of mine broke down within the first year. I remember thinking, *It's so good they have no children.* I didn't dare say that to him because, whether children are involved or not, the emotional impact of divorce is massive. There is no doubt though that it is far easier to have a clean break from a broken relationship when you have no children, as you won't need to constantly communicate with and see your ex-partner. However, it is also easier to ignore any personal issues which contributed to the break-down of the marriage in the first place. Ignoring those may make it more difficult to have a successful marriage in the future.

I was in a very fortunate place in life when Jenny and I separated. I ran my own business and so had flexibility with how I used my time. In addition, I had dissolved the business partnership and was already working from home. This meant I was able to give priority to looking after our kids. I understand that many men – probably most men – do not have this luxury. I have had many discussions with fathers going through a divorce who are not able to even contemplate a custody agreement where they would look after children during the week. This breaks my heart, not only for them, but also for their children.

As I mentioned earlier, Jenny and I came to a childcare arrangement early on. I looked after the kids from Thursday after school to Sunday night, and she cared for them from Sunday night till Thursday morning when she dropped them off at school. This arrangement worked initially. It was the best of a bad situation as I like to say and the kids were able to stay at the same school. We tried to keep most of their activities as normal and uninterrupted as possible, despite the fact that they had lost the security of living with the two most important people in their lives.

Early on, we had some mediation appointments with Relationships Australia. These provided very helpful information about what is 'best' for children in these circumstances. Below is a list of helpful points from the Relationship's Australia website relationships.org.au[2] for your reference:

- Assure them that both parents still love them, no matter what. You may have fallen out of love with their other parent, but the children still love that person and may not understand why you are separating.

- Give them a simple, honest account (but not one that blames or point scores against the other parent, or gives unnecessary detail). Explain who is moving away, and when and where they will see the other parent.

- Assure them that they do not have to take sides. They love both of you, so attacking or criticising the other parent hurts the children.

- Tell them this was an adult decision and that they are not to blame in any way. Draw a line between adult business and what children need to know.

- Try to make as few changes as possible in their lives.

- Let significant others know what is happening (ie. the school, class teacher, the parents of their friends). These people can also watch out for your children.

---

2. https://relationships.org.au/relationship-advice/relationship-advice-sheets/ending-a-relationship-1/children-and-separation

- NEVER use the children as go-betweens. Don't ask your children to deliver messages to the other parent or say negative things about the other parent. This is damaging to the child and reflects badly on you – children find it very difficult to deliver messages and don't want to be drawn into fights.

- Find a way to communicate politely and respectfully with your former partner and keep them informed about important matters regarding the children (health, injuries in your care, and education, for example).

- Be understanding if children play up or are distressed. Children need time and understanding as they adjust – many children are taken unawares when they hear their parents are separating and need a lot of assurance as they come to terms with the changes in their lives.

It is important to remember that all custody decisions involve two adults whose lives have been thrown into turmoil, and who are trying to establish new patterns and structures as they work out what life will look like moving forward. While Jenny and my custody issues were apparently resolved early, circumstances changed and we were faced with a disagreement about the custody of the children. People's situations change for a variety of reasons and any agreement needs to change with them. Here are just a few possible changes in circumstances based on discussions over the years with separated parents:

- One or both party wants greater or reduced custody.
- One of the parties wants to move their place of residence.
- One party has entered into a new relationship.
  This changes the dynamics of the whole situation.
- The children decide who they want to live with.
- The financial situation of one of the parties drives a change in custody arrangements.

There are undoubtedly many other reasons. At this point can I say very clearly:

> *... please consider the best interests of your children when making any decision about custody!!*

The fact that you are reading this chapter suggests that you are someone who puts the interests of your children before your own. If you do not, you may be grieved later when your children have no desire to spend time with you. That is a possible outcome, but not a guaranteed one. You may be happy having less time with your children. I certainly wasn't.

Many people gave me their opinion about what they thought was best for our children, many with the best intentions. They were showing concern and trying to be helpful. While their comments were often thought-provoking and occasionally helpful, some of them were just downright wrong.

I've heard many suggestions:

- Girls need their mother so they should live with her.
- Children need their mother so they should live with her.
- Boys need their father so they should live with him.
- Dads don't know how to care for children.
- It's better for the children to live primarily in one place.
- It's not good for children to live in two separate homes.
- Mums can spend your child support money on anything they want so it's best that the children live with you.

Reaching agreement about custody certainly differs depending on the age of the child/children. I am not qualified to hand out legal advice on such matters, but I believe there is no set age where a child can decide who they live with. If an agreement cannot be reached, either between the parents or through mediation, then you may have to leave it up to the courts to decide. My recommendation is that you seek to avoid that as far as it depends on you. Jenny and I were very fortunate to keep the matter of children custody and any other matters out of the court system.

There are a number of approaches when seeking to sort out custody:

- Come to a mutual agreement with your ex-spouse, either through one-on-one discussion or mediation.
- Discuss the options with your child/children and let them give input into the decision, regardless of how old they are. Caution must be observed in this approach! Remember, it's about the children not you!
- Engage a lawyer to liaise with your ex-spouse on your behalf, or with their lawyer.
- Fight for your desired custody decision in the courts.

While marriage breakdowns and children custody arrangements have many similarities and a similar process, every situation is unique because all marriages, couples and children are different.

Different circumstances require different solutions and different personalities require different management.

When it comes to different situations, do you recall the story of the men's support group in Chapter 3. Damian was not even given a chance to enter into custody discussions with his wife. His first course of action was to try and find his wife and children, but she was gone and the children with her. I can't even begin to imagine how painful that situation must have been for Damian.

At the other end of the spectrum, I remember a discussion with a father who suffered a bitter and hostile marriage breakdown. He wanted his ex-wife to pay for the pain and embarrassment she put him through. He believed she was not fit to mother their children and could not possibly accept the idea that she would have any custody. Obviously, we cannot know the ins and outs of everyone's situation, but it seemed very clear to me that his agenda was more about revenge, rather than the best interests of their children. Even if his wife had put him through the ringer and was a real cause of embarrassment for him, she still had a right as a mother to parent their children. There was no indication of physical or emotional harm to the children as a result of her parenting. This custody battle seemed based on his hurt and pain. I felt sad for the children. Eventually, after many, many thousands of dollars, the courts gave the majority of the custody to the father. That father has strained relationships with some of his children today.

Children are very perceptive. As they grow up, they start figuring things out for themselves. Before you make any custody decisions, think of how you want your relationship with your children to look in 20 years' time. That will help you make wise decisions about custody.

Whenever I was faced with a custody decision, I tried to go through a number of questions – even processing the answers on paper, trusting that I would make the best decision for my children.

Here are just a few of the questions I asked myself:

- Am I basing my decision on my emotions or on what I think is best for my children?

- Is it important for them to spend time with both their mum and dad?

- Is it important for them to spend equal time with their mum and dad?

- Is it important that they stay together as siblings?

- Is it better for them to live in one place or two?

- How will they cope if they don't see one of their parents?

- Will they be in a place of safety?
- Will they have their physical, emotional and spiritual needs met?
- Will they be taught about faith in God?
- Will they be able to be involved in extra-curricular activities like sport or music or whatever else they may show an interest in?
- What will I be able to manage as their father?

Only you know what questions are important to you and I encourage you to write your own list. Then, if the need arises, you will be able to process the decision, removing as much emotion as possible. Let's be under no illusion, often decisions of this nature need to be made when you are in a bad place emotionally. It is wise to check your decision with someone safe and trustworthy before you action it.

Once you've made your decision, then you need to work through all the issues with your ex-spouse – as amicably as possible. If all goes well, you will arrive at a mutual decision that is best for your children – and fair to both parents. If that process does not go well, then you need to decide what is worth fighting for and what you can let go of.

Thankfully, Jenny and I were able to keep custody issues out of the courts and lock in a shared custody agreement. I did have to let go of some things I wanted, without any detriment to the wellbeing of our children or any long-term negative impacts on their future.

The shared custody document is signed by both parties, either prepared by yourselves from a template obtained from a solicitor, or prepared by solicitors/lawyers. Our custody agreement resulted in 50/50 shared care of the children with a week on, week off arrangement. When the children were older, they chose what their living arrangements looked like. In Chapter 10, our children provide some great insights into the impact of custody issues on them.

Discussion Starters

- Children are the innocent victims of divorce.

- Think of the children when communicating with your ex-spouse.

- When it comes to decisions that need to be made now, think of the long-term impact on your relationship with your children.

- Allow trusted and safe people to affirm your decisions.

Surviving Divorce – A New Beginning

SIX

Learning And Recovering

After my divorce I found myself asking questions such as:

- What sort of husband was I?
- What sort of father was I?
- Why did I get married in the first place?

So many more questions.

Gaining an understanding of the role I played in the breakdown of my marriage was a very confronting part of my recovery from the divorce. Working through such questions is not a compulsory part of divorce recovery. You can recover without this soul-searching, but avoiding it will impact a number of things: how well you recover; your future relationships with your children and others; and the success of any future marital relationship.

When I talk with people who have gone through marital separation, I find varying degrees of willingness to learn from the past, but I believe that giving yourself time and space for such evaluations may help you avoid repeating past mistakes. Mind you, putting your whole life on hold and spending the next ten years evaluating the breakup is not a healthy option either. While we may want to have all the issues worked through and resolved before entering into another relationship, that is unlikely to be the reality. Personal development is a life-long journey.

Let me tell you about Paul whose marriage separation was troubled. He loved his wife deeply and found the separation hard. They had three children in their late teens who spent most of the time in his care. Paul's need for another partner was very strong. In less than 12 months he decided to look for another companion via a dating site. Paul chose a Christian dating site and felt he had that box ticked off quite nicely. Now don't get me wrong, I'm certainly not against dating websites; I know couples who have very successful marriages after finding one another on a dating website. The issue here is not the dating website, but the time Paul left between the marriage separation and his search for a replacement companion. Perhaps that was exactly what he was looking for – a replacement companion. He found someone and they married in a very short time. Unfortunately, their marriage lasted less than six months. I want you to imagine the additional impact on teenagers who had just been through the separation of their parents. Paul did not take time to evaluate potential past mistakes. Sadly, Paul and his family have now endured additional subsequent marriage breakdowns.

Regardless of the reasons for a marriage breakdown, we can always learn something about the role we have played in it. 'But I didn't do anything to cause the breakdown!' I hear you say. That's what I told myself initially too, but it's important not to focus on blame, but rather on possible causes. Through God's grace and, trust me, I needed and still need His grace, I have been able to accept the fact that a number of things in my 'makeup' contributed to the marriage breakdown.

I found that the evaluation process can take you back to your childhood as you seek to answer the question, 'Why did I get married in the first place?' You may be thinking, 'Well, it's too late to ask that question NOW!' It may be too late for your broken marriage, but not for any future relationship. Remember, this is not just about recovering from a broken marriage. It is also about being able to thrive in future relationships, perhaps even a future marriage!

I have said it before and I will say it again

....

...it takes time to work through the issues.

....

Working through any issues thoroughly is much easier without the distraction of another relationship. I don't believe we need to have everything 'sorted' before we enter into another relationship, but working through some of the key aspects which contributed to the marriage breakdown certainly helps. From a faith viewpoint, giving God time to reveal truths and begin the healing process was important for me. I say *begin* the healing process because I have found that healing is a life-long journey of learning and discovery. You and only you can decide how long this process is going to take or needs to take.

What are some of the key questions to ask yourself as you go through this learning process? Here are just a few which I wrestled with. Some I spent a little time considering; others took significant time:

- Why did I get married?
- Was my focus on my wife fulfilling my needs or did I focus on fulfilling her needs?
- Did I give the time to the marriage that I needed to?
- Did I put anyone else before my marriage?
- Why did I want to have children?
- Did I model being a good husband to my children?
- Was my wife more important to me than God?
- What could I have done differently which may have resulted in a successful marriage?
- What is my understanding of love?
- Did I truly love her?

Wow, these are big questions – heavy stuff. Not the sort of process that can be worked through in a couple of weeks, not even months.

I must say again as someone who has gone through the divorce process, it is a lot easier to work on a marriage than to work on a divorce – especially if children are involved. After the divorce, I often wondered, *If I'd asked myself these questions while I was married, would my marriage have survived?* Certainly, the answers would have given me deeper insight into the state of my marriage. If your marriage is hemorrhaging, pondering these questions may give you the insight needed to save your marriage. The answers to these questions certainly helped me when I re-married.

Now, speaking as a 'bloke', most of us seem to think that we can work through such a process on our own. That may very well be possible, but doesn't seem wise or ideal. And, while it is widely accepted that women receive advice and instruction more readily than men, this is not always the case. I know a number of divorced women who simply refuse to listen to advice . A wonderful Bible proverb says, 'Those who ignore instruction despise themselves, but he who listens to correction gains understanding' (Proverbs 15:32 ESV translation). Suck it up guys and gals, getting through a divorce is a lot easier with the wise counsel of others. Why do you think I am writing this book?

I was very fortunate. God brought into my life many wise people with great insight at just the right time to assist in my recovery process. I had a very wise and godly mother who was a great sounding board and support. In addition, a wise older Christian couple took me under their wing. I also had a spiritually discerning uncle and aunt, a caring and non-intrusive counsellor and pastor, and some good friends with whom I could talk. God played a massive part throughout the whole process.

Despite all this assistance, my role was central and indispensable. I needed to ...

- Be open to instruction and correction. I know, I know ... you have done nothing wrong, but trust me on this one. It's vital!
- Be prepared to be honest and frank with others.
- Trust people.
- Get out of my place of comfort.
- Swallow my pride and allow others to help.
- Be willing to share my experiences.
- Let go of misguided prejudices.
- Look beyond the faults and mistakes of others and love them.

Learning And Recovering

What sort of help is available to you? Who could you turn to? Below are various possibilities. If you are a person of faith, the first option is not an option, but a necessity.

- Take your issues to God and then spend time listening to what He has to say. This is vitally important folks!!
- Seek out trusted and safe friend/s who can listen well. Allowing them to talk into your situation is a bonus.
- Use written resources which speak into each stage of your recovery. Hopefully this book will help, but there are many other options out there. Relationships Australia have great resources about a range of relationship issues.
- Find a counsellor. A trusted friend may be able to recommend one. If possible, see someone who is not counselling any of your close friends or family. If you are not comfortable with that counsellor, look for someone else!
- Don't limit yourself to the Christian community or a community environment you are familiar with. Assistance promoted as Christian may not always be helpful for you.
- Initially make sure you surround yourself with 'safe' people.
- Have I said make sure those around you are 'safe' people?
- And finally, **surround yourself with 'safe' people!**

Remember this is not about perfect recovery, but about recovering well so that you are equipped for more fulfilling and lasting relationships in the future.

Discussion Starters

- Give yourself time to learn and recover.

- Allow God to talk into your situation.
  Are you willing to listen?

- Surround yourself with safe and trusted people.

- And remember, you will recover – wonderful, meaningful relationships await you.

SEVEN

Communicating With Your Ex-Spouse

Remember June's husband, 'Peter', from the Introduction? When I think about speaking well of your ex-partner, Peter immediately comes to mind. Peter and June's separation was not a pleasant experience for either of them. Peter was particularly hurt, yet as I got to know him and he talked about his relationship with June, Peter's humility and kindness became very evident. He talked about her with a beautiful warmth, even though their marriage was over. Despite his hurt, he spoke of her as a committed mother and wife. Perhaps Peter was in denial, but he looked beyond the failings of others and offered forgiveness beyond what the world understands. He was a man of faith. His attitude was, *Who am I to judge when I know my own wretchedness, and have a God who is willing to love and forgive me regardless?* I was humbled and learnt a lot from him. Peter is happily remarried now. You, like me, may be thinking, *Well, there's no way I could do that!* That's OK. We don't have to, but it is helpful if we can.

There are countless examples of the other end of the spectrum where betrayal leads to domestic violence, even sometimes tragically to loss of life. The effects of divorce are bad enough, but adding murder or suicide into the equation deeply impacts children and others, and helps to undermine a healthy society. Having said that, the deep, deep pain separation brings to men and women, can lead to extreme reactions and unpredictable behaviour. The pain runs deep and the recovery process can be long, but it is possible to come out the other side. I believe we should all be striving for healthy communication and eventual recovery.

When no children are involved, communication with an ex-partner can be cut off completely. However, immediately after the separation there are almost always practical issues that need to be dealt with. This will require communication, unless it is all done through a third party. I found it very helpful to view all communication with my ex-wife, especially at the early and emotionally raw stage of the process, as a business transaction. As sad as that sounds, it enabled me to distance myself as much as possible from the emotional side of decision making and I believe resulted in a more beneficial outcome for the whole family. I would love to say that this was easy to do and that I succeeded in every circumstance, but I would be lying.

The level of communication required varies greatly with different circumstances. If the separation is amicable rather than hostile, communication may be no problem at all. If children are not involved, interactions with your ex-partner after separation may be minimal. That is not necessarily a bad thing. If children are involved, you may be communicating on a regular basis, especially if you have a shared custody arrangement. To be frank, if you have a shared custody arrangement, then

> *...communicating as amicably as possible is a must if you have the best interests of your children in mind.*

You might be thinking, *But he betrayed me in ways that are unforgivable! You just don't understand how hard it is to hear his voice and not want to throw up.* I am sincerely sorry if that is your situation, but using the recommendations in the previous chapter may help you engage in positive ways with your ex-partner and will reap benefits for everyone, including you.

I am reminded of Benjamin, whose marriage dissolved while their three children were in their early and late teens. Benjamin was very committed to his marriage and expected the same level of commitment from his wife.

When the relationship broke down, pain and grief hit Benjamin very hard. He was unable to do the self-evaluation that would have helped him reach a better understanding of what had happened. His inability to forgive his ex-wife had serious consequences on their interactions and on their children. Unfortunately, Benjamin was unable to communicate at all with his ex-wife because the pain was too great (no judgement or condemnation from me dear friend). This hurt their children deeply – hurts they will have to process as they journey through life without their father's input. I am not saying a certain level of recovery needs to be achieved to be able to move forward, but there is no question in my mind that the more we are prepared to work through any issues, the better will be the outcome for everyone, not least for ourselves.

Depending on the age of your children at the time of separation, there may be significant events which will require you to be in the same place as your ex-spouse. Here are just some of the events which may necessitate communication with your ex-spouse. To my surprise, I showed up at some of these events having completely forgotten that Jenny would be there. I was totally unprepared when I saw her. So, at the risk of pointing out the bleeding obvious, you may confront one another at:

- Birthday celebrations.
- Special gatherings for Christmas or Easter or other special holidays.
- 18th and 21st birthday parties.
- Weddings and funerals.
- Baptisms.
- Extended family gatherings.
- Graduations.
- Sporting events.
- Musical performances, etc.

Such times, although initially awkward, can still be wonderful celebrations – and should be for the sake of your children.

I remember our son Leo's 21st birthday. We held the celebration at my and my now wife's home. Leo was living with us at the time. It was a bizarre experience seeing my first wife Jenny and my second wife Lorraine, in the kitchen preparing food for the guests together. I very clearly remember asking God, 'How does this work Lord?' It was a wonderful blessing for our children to have both their parents attend one celebration for Leo's 21st. I give Jenny credit for being prepared to put herself in a foreign environment where she knew very few people for the benefit of our children. Mind you, it took a few years to get to that stage and we both had our struggles along the way, but we can see the benefits in the kids' lives. There have also been a few occasions where we met in a café with all three children for a specific celebration. I confess that still, to this day, I find this awkward, but know just how important it is to our children. We have no illusions about the past, but also understand that life can still be celebrated together.

Remember that the journey can always be picked up again and many wrongs righted. I don't believe it is ever too late for the restoration of broken relationships. I am not only talking about broken marriages, but broken relationships in general.

Let me give you some very simple truths that I have learnt:

- The breakdown of relationship always involves at least two people.
- Both people will have contributed in some way to that breakdown.
- It takes two willing people to make a marriage work and it takes two willing people to reconcile a marriage – or end it amicably.
- You are not responsible for your spouse's decisions.
- Forgiveness allows you to be set free.

As I pointed out earlier, your circumstances have a significant impact on communication with your ex-spouse. One such circumstance is another man or woman coming on the scene and the manner in which they come.

It's one thing to have a marriage fail, and to lose the relationship with the person you love and want to spend the rest of your life with. It is quite another thing when that person starts a relationship with someone else. Wow! How do you deal with that? From what I have seen, regardless of how old they are

> *... there is a very high possibility that your ex-spouse will start a new relationship – and may even remarry.*

This may be too hard for you to contemplate right now. If so, please stop reading and come back to this at another time, if and when you are ready.

When I found out that my ex-wife was seeing someone, I was dreading the first time I would need to interact with them. As it turned out, I wasn't prepared when it finally happened. It was sprung on me completely by surprise one Christmas Day. The kids were with Jenny for the morning and I was to pick them up from Jenny's house in the early afternoon so they could spend the rest of Christmas Day with me. I approached the exchange as I normally would, planning to be polite and say hello. I wouldn't go inside because that was just too awkward at this stage. I parked in the street as I normally did and got out of my car, walked to the front door and knocked. To my surprise Jenny's new friend, Ben, opened the door. To make matters worse, I was at the bottom of the steps standing about half a metre below him, with his face about one meter from mine. HELLO! I was caught completely by surprise. I was expecting Jenny to open the door.

All I can remember is saying, 'G'day mate, is Jenny there?'

He said something like, 'Yeh, I'll just go get her.'

Jenny came to the door with Leo, Makayla and Brooke and I said to them, 'Go jump in the car while I talk to mum.'

Ben stayed in the doorway with his arm around Jenny the whole time, looking extremely angry to me. He didn't say anything – just stood there. I finished my discussion with Jenny and went to join the kids.

As I jumped in the car, Leo, who would have been about eight at the time and very perceptive said, 'Dad did you see the look on Ben's face? He looked so angry. Why?'

'I don't know Leo', I replied – and honestly, I didn't know.

Later God revealed that this was Ben's default defense mechanism. He was afraid of what I might say or do, so he was protecting himself by trying to intimidate me. Over time I actually had some interesting discussions with Ben and our relationship, while by no means a friendship, was at least polite. Again, regardless of what I thought of him or their friendship, for the benefit of my children I tried to keep the lines of communication open and respectful. I have to be honest and confess that for many years I struggled with seeing my ex-wife and Ben together. Praise God, I have been able to let go of many things relating to those interactions. I never went out of my way to establish a relationship with Ben but eventually, when we met, there was no obvious awkwardness.

I know of another separated Christian couple who quite deliberately interact and have social gatherings involving just them and their new husband and wife. If separated couples are able to manage that for the good of their children, then I think it is a great place to get to.

Once again, I must emphasise that all situations are different and will be managed in different ways. What is the 'best' way? I suggest ways which enable all parties to maintain healthy and safe relationships with one another. Remember guys and gals, as far as I am concerned there is no right or wrong way here. The aim is to find what works for each of us in our situation.

You may like to refer back to Chapter 5 for Relationships Australia's suggestions about communicating with your ex-spouse.

Discussion Starters

- Try to put your own pain aside.
- Look to the future and avoid bringing up the past.
- Good communication will benefit your children and your relationship with them in the long run.
- Prepare yourself to meet and communicate with your ex-spouse when attending gatherings where this is likely.
- Expect surprise meetings.
- Prepare yourself for your ex-spouse to enter into a new relationship at some stage.

EIGHT

Finances

A husband and wife bring to the marriage partnership skillsets which benefit (or hamper) the marriage and the children born from that marriage. Each plays a particular role within the marriage and hopefully both will benefit. The tasks of managing a household, educating, feeding and raising children, providing spiritual guidance, emotional and physical counsel, and financial stability for the family are hopefully shared – ideally in an environment of love and servanthood. This is marriage as designed by God. Sadly, divorce splits that partnership. These tasks are no longer shared by two loving people, but are often duplicated with both people having to play all roles at different times, in different locations and in different ways. The financial impact of divorce on both parties is significant.

Lisa was in her mid-thirties when she separated from her husband in 2002. They still had a debt of $90,000 on the family home which was valued at $130,000. They had one car and other small debts. Lisa and her husband had four young children. Lisa was a full-time stay-at-home mum, relying on her husband's income to meet all their financial needs. Lisa had a good understanding of money and was responsible for managing their finances. The circumstance of the separation forced Lisa to seek alternative accommodation and to care for their four children. She now had to manage a household and provide financially. As Lisa's husband chose not to work after the separation, she initially received minimal child support of $40 a month – not a sustainable situation.

At times like this some well-meaning Christian brothers and sisters may say, 'It will be OK. God will provide.' While this may be true, such comments are very unhelpful. Lisa was fortunate. She had a wonderful support network of family and friends. Lisa and her children were able to stay with her parents for a short time while she got herself sorted, emotionally and financially. We are so fortunate in this 'lucky' country of Australia with a government which provides financial assistance for people in Lisa's situation. Lisa was eligible for about $500 financial assistance a week from the government through their assistance support programs.

If you find yourself in a similar predicament, start by contacting Services Australia or visit their website www.servicesaustralia.gov.au and search for 'Separated parents' options. This website is a wonderful resource for many issues relating to parenting, including financial assistance. Lisa and her husband were both left with about $10,000 cash after a 50% split of all assets. Lisa used $7,000 of that to purchase a car. When I asked Lisa how she survived financially, she said she managed her budget.

Ah yes, budget! How do you budget? I strongly suggest you seek advice from either a trusted friend who has a good understanding of finance or a professional who understands the predicament you now find yourself in.

Let me give a very simple starting point for budgeting. I use a month-by-month spreadsheet starting with January and finishing with December (unlike a financial year budget as used in a business). I have included a very simple sample budget on the following page. It is broken into two sections: expenses and income.

Finances

Year

	Jan	Feb	Mar	Apr	May	Jun	Jul	Aug	Sep	Oct	Nov	Dec	**TOTAL $**
Expense Items													
Books, CDs and DVDs													
Council Rates													
Dining out and takeaway													
Electricity and gas													
Entertainment, pay TV													
Gardening & tools													
Gifts to others													
Groceries													
Health insurance													
Holidays													
Homeware													
Mortgage/rent													
Tithes & donations													
Water													
White goods & furniture													
Parent Clothing													
General													
Children Clothing													
Schooling													
General													
Public transport													
Subscriptions & registration													
Telephone & internet													
Vehicle Fuel													
Insurance & rego													
Repair													
Other													
TOTALS													

Income

	Jan	Feb	Mar	Apr	May	Jun	Jul	Aug	Sep	Oct	Nov	Dec	**TOTAL $**
Work													
Other													
TOTAL													
Income minus Expenses													

I always start with my expenses and what I call the 'essentials': the items required to survive such as groceries, rent, clothing and health needs. Once I deal with these I move onto other very important expenses such as transport: fuel, car registration, public transport. If you have children, you may need to provide separate categories for them. To keep things very simple you can use single combined categories for the whole family. Once I have essentials and very important expenses covered, I move onto the less essential categories such as entertainment, dining out, leisure activities, etc. Everyone's list will look different.

The reason I use a budget is to gain an understanding of what my income needs are: first to survive, and then to see what type of lifestyle I may be able to afford. Lisa understood this. Early on she received financial assistance from friends: a small gift hamper here, a small cash donation there. People gave because they saw a need, not because Lisa asked for financial help.

If you isolate yourself from everyone, you do not give others the opportunity to bless you with sound advice and generosity.

Many separated women have told me about the unfortunate situations they have endured – situations where the father of their children met few or none of his financial obligations. I have also spoken to a number of men who proudly brag that they didn't pay any child support to their ex-wife after the separation. I don't sit in judgement on these men, but I do feel for their ex-wives and children.

Many ex-wives endure lives of fear and financial uncertainty. Many children, through no fault of their own, in addition to the separation of their parents, also deal with serious emotional and physical consequences. Some mothers are unable to adequately feed their families, let alone enable them to be part of a sporting team or dance group. Many children wear clothes that are too small or wear shoes with holes – and there is definitely no pocket money for treats. These children can become increasingly isolated and withdrawn. I am yet to hear that the fathers of these children – often men with selfish and revengeful attitudes – have close relationships with their children. This situation can only lead to resentment, bitterness and further fracturing of relationships. 'Yes, preach it brother,' I hear the ladies saying, and for good reason.

There is a flip side to the picture I have just drawn. This involves a loving father and husband who now finds himself on his own, often with very limited access to his children, yet still having to work hard to provide for them. He has no say in how his hard-earned money is spent. It may be spent on the needs of his children who are under the care of his ex-wife, or on his ex-wife's weekend away with the new partner while a friend looks after the children. Does that sound ridiculous? I'm afraid that, after many conversations over the years, nothing surprises me anymore about people's ability to ignore responsibilities and seek their own happiness – or revenge.

I have also seen fathers, in particular, change their employment to avoid paying child support to their ex-wife. I see mothers trying to get as much of their ex-husband's money and assets as possible, seeking revenge for the marriage separation. I have seen children seriously neglected, even though child support payments are made for the specific benefit of the child/children. As far as I am aware there is no requirement for child support payments to be spent on the children, a situation which must be resented by the person paying for their children's welfare. I suggest that the best outcome is an agreement which clearly states what will be paid and by whom, specifically for support of any children. At times, this seems to be unachievable. For some couples engaging lawyers and solicitors to assist them in reaching an agreement is simply too expensive. You do have the option to represent yourself through the legal process, and there are organisations which can provide assistance to varying levels: some free of charge, some for minimal costs and some for substantial fees. I am reluctant to make a recommendation because all situations are different and all experiences with such organisations vary. Suffice to say, do your homework and find an organisation which suits your situation.

I have shared Lisa's financial experience, which I suggest, is probably very common. My own experience of the financial impact of divorce is perhaps more unusual. Before our family trip to Queensland when I suspected that my marriage was in trouble, Jenny and I owned our own home and had no debt. This was 2004, we were in our early to mid-30s and our assets were worth approximately $400,000. We had two cars and a very comfortable life style; we were free to spend money and to travel as we chose.

By the time our divorce was finalised and all paperwork signed, we each walked away with about $60,000 in cash. We both had a car and our other possessions were distributed fairly. Jenny had a job and I had a business, so we were both earning an income and were able to care for our children in separate homes. I found letting go of much of what we'd worked for over nine years and starting again a very bitter pill to swallow. In addition, I had to provide financial support to Jenny. Needless to say, I did a fair bit of grumbling, but decided to take a very simple approach to my financial situation. God had provided all we needed before (and plenty extra) and He would continue to provide all that my children and I needed.

Jenny and I came to a verbal agreement that I would assist her financially, paying for all expenses relating directly to the children when they were in her care. This meant all our children's educational and extra curricula activities (sport etc.) were being provided for. As time went on, we began to follow the financial requirements for shared custody outlined by the Australian Government. If you are concerned about your ability to survive financially, a good place to start is with the Federal Government website. The amount of child support paid by either parent at the time of my separation was determined using a calculation based on the income of the parents and the level of custody each parent was responsible for. It is also worth remembering that, when it comes to child support calculations, new partners and their children are not included.

Lisa's story shows a situation where one of the parties fails to meet their financial obligations after a divorce, leaving the other party in a dire financial situation. As with all decisions made in a divorce settlement, the financial aspects need to be made with the long-term situation in mind. I highlight once again, if children are involved then

... consider the long-term relationships you want to have with your children.

Lisa's ex-husband has no communication or relationship with any of his four children.

The previous chapter covered communication with your ex-spouse. The advice given there is relevant when seeking to reach a mutually acceptable financial settlement. You definitely don't want your ex-spouse bad-mouthing you to the kids for valid reasons, so be very careful about financial decisions that may adversely impact your children's welfare. Remember, as your children grow they will judge for themselves how well the financial side of your divorce was handled and assess its impact on their lives. I want my children's final verdict to be, 'Thank you Dad for the way you handled that!'

The complexity of financial matters relating to divorce makes it very easy to become disheartened, especially when you feel that you have been treated unfairly. Many will also find financial matters confusing and difficult. My words of assurance may ring hollow, but taking time to work through the network of support options will provide some level of assistance and reassurance. I found government organisations such as Legal Aid (www.legalaid.vic.gov.au), Services Australia (www.servicesaustralia.gov.au) and Family Relationships (www.familyrelationships.gov.au) very helpful.

You may have to swallow some humble pie and ask for help.

You do not have to try to work through it all yourself. It may be that your life-style will have to change. The information about evaluation and recovery from the previous chapter may be helpful here. Working out what is important to you is a great way to get things in perspective and can often help you realise that what you thought was a very difficult financial situation is not so bad after all. You may have to initially forget about the weekly restaurant meal or the two-week holiday you are used to taking every year. We have all heard the saying 'short term pain for long term gain'. That certainly rings true in this situation. Careful management of your new financial situation and adjustment of your lifestyle will build a positive outlook on your future.

Even when children are not involved, the pain and sense of loss is no less real. A dear friend of mine, Hayden, lost his marriage after only 18 months. This was nothing short of devastating for him. The emotional heartache was deepened by the reality of significant financial losses. It was a real battle for him. The equal distribution of their financial assets started to become an ever-increasing burden, even an obsession for Hayden. Given the manner in which his marriage ended, it became increasingly important that a fair split of their possessions was achieved. It became apparent that this distribution process was a large part of his grief over the loss of his marriage. It was no longer about the money, but about his ability to let go of the perceived injustice. "why should I have to give up something that was not the result of my choice?" I remember receiving a number of phone calls from him. He was in a state of distress, not knowing how to react to the number of shares to be distributed between him and his ex-wife. The amount was quite insignificant in the overall scheme of things, but Hayden's desire for justice outweighed the monetary value of the shares.

It is important not to allow events and circumstances that are insignificant assume disproportionate importance because we are overwhelmed and driven by our emotions. Thankfully, after evaluating his priorities and long-term goals, Hayden was able to release the decision about those shares to God. It then became a non-issue – a win win for everyone. If only things always worked out that way.

Discussion Starters

- Don't isolate yourself from your trusted friends.
- Don't make rash decisions when experiencing powerful emotions.
- Allow others to assist you financially.
- Seek wise counsel in relation to your finances and any other important decisions.
- Consider the long-term impact of your decisions.
- Think about your long-term relationship with your children before acting.
- Be prepared to change your lifestyle.

Surviving Divorce – A New Beginning

NINE

Communicating With Your Children

Our children – the innocent victims in this ugly mess called divorce. I have often cried with men and women over the impact divorce has had on their children – and on my own. Please do me a favour. Regardless of what stage you are at: in a healthy marriage, in a struggling marriage, temporarily separated, long-term separated or divorced, just sit back and think of each of your children.

- How old are they?
- What do you admire about them?
- What about them makes you smile – even laugh with joy?
- What do they like to do?
- What do you like doing with them and they with you?
- Now, how do you picture them in two years, five years, 20 years' time?

My eyes fill with tears as I write this and think of my own children. A broken marriage will have a significant impact on the life of any children involved. Don't kid yourself and think that this isn't necessarily true. Sorry to be so blunt, but it is the truth. Can your children recover from the trauma of divorce? Of course they can, but your ability to manage your divorce well will have a massive impact on how well your children recover. Just in case you missed it, while you ponder the wonderful uniqueness of your child/children:

> *Your ability to manage your divorce well has a massive impact on the recovery of your children.*

You might be thinking, *but I didn't ask for this situation or cause it!* That may be so, but your behaviour, during and after your divorce, will have a huge impact on your children's ability to recover well. I am so looking forward to seeing what contribution my children make to this book in the next chapter. Wait! Hang on! Maybe I'm not. What if they tell you I stuffed up? What if their pain is laid bare for all to see and I am the cause of some of it – even much of it?

I got so sick and tired of hearing, 'Don't worry about your kids! They're very resilient.'

This comment provided a small level of comfort at the time but, despite people's reassurance, I tried hard to keep the impact of the divorce on my kids at the forefront when making decisions. This helped me to keep a proper perspective, and to make decisions based on long-term goals and desires, rather than simply on the here and now.

My kids were quite young at the time of our separation. Leo was seven, Makayla was six and Brooke was four. There is no doubt in my mind that the separation had a serious impact on them at a level I couldn't understand at the time, and they could not possibly have understood. How do I know this? I remember Makayla forming the habit of licking her lips to the point where they were always red and started to break into sores. This was how she expressed her anxiety.

It broke my heart when she came to me one day and said, 'Daddy, my heart hurts. Why does my heart hurt?'

Here come the tears yet again. How could I possibly answer that? I sat and talked with her about what it meant for her to have parents who no longer lived together. I then thought it may be helpful for her to talk to a professional counsellor. She did, but it became clear that children need their parents' help more than help from anyone or anything else.

My children's journey of recovery was slow. Even now, new issues are being revealed for my children as they move through their early 20s. I am sure questions, realisations and long-term impacts will continue to surface for the rest of their lives.

We see so much addiction in our society as a means of coping with life: drugs, alcohol, pornography, prostitution; the list goes on. None of these are healthy means of coping. We can't always control how our children choose to cope, but we can encourage positive coping mechanisms, such as sports, hobbies, socialising, music, art and even simple tears.

I know a woman, now 30 years old, whose parents separated and divorced when she was about 15. She expressed her emotional grief through her artwork. Not long after the divorce of her parents, she created a number of very dark and scary paintings and sculptures which spoke directly about the pain and grief she was suffering and, in some ways, continues to suffer. These works did not invoke emotions of joy and happiness, but it was such a blessing that she was able to release her emotions in that way. Over time her artwork showed a very clear path of recovery and healing. It now speaks of joy, hope and expectations of a positive future. She is now very happily married with four children.

We cannot control how our children choose to manage their emotional pain and grief. But we can do our best to support them, communicate with them and seek to provide a safe place for them to recover and move forward. It is a real joy to be able to encourage your child to step out into the real world and become their own person, follow their own dreams and live the life God has planned for them.

In Chapter 5 we looked at making decisions about child custody. The manner in which we communicate with our children has a significant impact on their ability to cope. Now let's consider some of the impacts that various custody situations can have on children. I am no child psychologist, so my views on this matter come from my experience with seven children: my three and the four children of my now wife of 11 years, Lorraine. In addition, I have had discussions with many other separated couples and their children.

It is important to re-iterate the importance of parents putting aside their differences and their pain, as best they can, when communicating with their children. No matter how angry you are with your ex-partner and how negatively you view their parenting, your children still love them. I have witnessed children defending parents who have said and done horrific things to them. Now let me be very clear. In my opinion, the physical and emotional abuse of children is not to be accepted or tolerated in any form. If you see evidence of such behavior, you owe it to your children to remove them from that environment. The law may even require it.

What I am suggesting is that you refuse to pass on and burden your children with your personal disappointments and sadness. The honest truth is that you may often do this without realising that you are doing so. That is why it is so important to have close, trusted friends who will honestly speak into your situation. You need friends who are prepared to pick you up on any behavior which is not in the best interests of your children. When they do that, try not to defend or excuse your behavior. Remember the wisdom of Proverbs 19:20. 'Listen to advice and accept instruction, that you may gain wisdom in the future' (English Standard Version).

Here are some keys points about communicating with your younger children through the difficult separation period. As they get older, your communication levels will need to change, although some of these points apply whatever the age of your children.

- Never put down the other parent in front of the children.

- Never talk about specific reasons for the separation in front of the children.

- Allow your children to express how they are feeling without becoming defensive.

- Always provide a safe environment and sufficient time for your children to communicate. Remember, they may be ready to talk at a time that is very inconvenient to you, but it's important to listen.

- Never try to justify your behaviour to your children. They will see right through you (especially if they are a nine-year-old girl named Brooke! Let's not go there!)

- Remember your children will always see themselves, you and your ex-spouse as their 'family', even if you have both remarried.

What about older kids? The way you communicate with them can and perhaps should be quite different. If they are in their late teens, remember that they will have a far better understanding of the apparent injustice that has been thrust upon them than if they are younger. They may well see for themselves much of what has happened and need to process and make sense of it all.

I have seen first-hand with Lorraine the agonising process of not being able to 'fix' the suffering of teenage children. In reality we are unable to 'fix' things for any child, but being able to sit down calmly and talk through things is often far easier with younger children. This is a huge generalisation. So many factors, including personality and maturity, impact communication with older children. If you know your children well, you will know what works best for them. If you find it hard to really know and understand your children, rest assured that – if you take time to communicate well with them – you will get to know them a whole lot better during the recovery process.

What I have observed with older children in a range of different situations is:

- They will often approach us when they want answers.
- When they want an answer, they generally want it there and then.
- We need to be very patient with them through the whole process.
- They will know when you are fumbling for the right answer.
- They can see through any dishonesty.
- They have a good understanding of justice. Many younger children do too.
- Their emotional battle is either very private or on display for all to see.

- They will shut down if the environment is not safe for them.
- If you don't come to the party and seek to meet their emotional needs, they will look elsewhere. Parents beware!!

There is a common theme regardless of the age of your children at the time of separation and through the recovery process. When you are communicating with your children IT IS NOT ABOUT YOU! Having your own recovery support network in place, enables you to provide more support to your children.

They need you to be there for them as a major player, if not the most important player, in their recovery network.

I look back at the father I was during my first marriage and am honestly appalled by how I failed in some areas. I could give you a long list of justifications for my choices and behaviour. I could give lots of reasons why I did the things I did and assure you that it wasn't my fault. I could tell you that I did the best I could. All that may very well be true, but it doesn't change the fact that there were shortcomings that negatively impact my children to this day.

Can I be so bold as to suggest that we all have those burdens of failure. I am not saying that to make myself feel better, even though it does in some small pathetic way. We are simply part of a fallen world and we will never have it all together. And you know what? Even though that is OK, we can always be striving to do things better. My marriage separation helped me become a better father in ways that may not have occurred if we had stayed married. Wow, what a call! If only the 'being a better father' thing was able to happen while staying married. Regardless of your situation, do you want to be a better father or mother? My prayer is that your answer is a resounding 'YES!' My challenge is, what are you going to do about it?

May I be so bold to suggest that you start by stopping and listening to your children regardless of their age. Not just listen – look right into their eyes as you listen so they know they have your undivided attention. What you do after that is driven by what they have said.

After my divorce, I remember sitting in my comfy couch in my tiny lounge room facing the passage, while my two gorgeous daughters, aged 5 and 7, put on a dancing and recital show for me. It was as if they were performing to a thousand strong audience, but it was only me, their daddy. They felt so special – and so did I.

Stop and give your children your undivided attention!

I want to share some of the fears I had for my children resulting from my marriage breakup – fears which 17 years later have proved to have no foundation. Some of my fears were:

- My kids wouldn't survive this situation.
- They wouldn't be able to have a great marriage themselves.
- They would think the divorce was their fault.
- I wouldn't be able to see them very often.
- They would be embarrassed by me.
- They wouldn't be able to see what a good marriage looks like.

It was important for me to allow God to speak truth into these lies. The lies were repeated over and over – and each time God needed once again to show me the truth. Eventually that lying voice was mostly silent as my relationships with my children grew stronger and I learned the value of being available whenever they needed me to listen. It is truly not about us. It is about them!

Discussion Starters

- Each of your children is unique.
- It is important to create a safe place where they can share their thoughts and feelings with you.
- Don't take anything they say too personally.
- Understand where the comments are coming from, especially if they come from their pain.
- They love your ex-spouse just as much as they love you.

TEN

Through The Eyes Of Children

I had no intention of asking my children to be involved or contribute to this book in any way. I didn't want to force them to re-visit any of the experiences or emotions they have had to endure through the divorce process. I did however feel it was very important that they were aware that I was planning to write this book. They feature in many of the stories and were likely to want to read it at some stage, so I made sure they were comfortable before I began writing. To my surprise, my youngest daughter Brooke who was 19 years old at the time, asked if she could contribute to the book. What a great idea – if rather confronting! I was sure she had gathered much wisdom as she journeyed with divorced parents. It was only fair to offer the same opportunity to Leo and Makayla. They too were happy to contribute.

The intention for this book is exactly what the title *Surviving Divorce* suggests, and that applies to our children as well. I asked Leo (24), Makayla (23) and Brooke (21) to write whatever they wanted and felt would be helpful to other parents and children living with divorce. Their responses have been edited (not by me), but have not been modified. It reads as it was and is for them.

I asked them three questions:

1. What was the most difficult aspect of having your parents separate?

2. What do you see as the pros and cons of living in the shared custody of both parents? Would you have preferred to live with just one parent?

3. What do you wish your parents had done differently after the divorce?

Below are their reflections on these questions.

1. What was the most difficult aspect of having your parents separate?

Leo

Looking back, I think one of the most difficult aspects of living with divorced parents was a non-uniform lifestyle. The living environment at each home was very different. Each parent had different views, ideals and teachings. Being taught to live one way was a thing of the past – I was now living two lives.

Living with divorced parents made it very difficult for me to become the best possible version of myself. So many aspects of life, such as what each parent would tolerate, their expectations and what I could or couldn't get away with were different. There was no clarity about the right path forward; it was like standing at a fork in the road split into many routes. This led to much uncertainty about myself and my decisions. My living environment wasn't linear; it was sinusoidal.

- Church one week, no church the other.
- Bedtime at 8pm or 12am.
- Living with four step-siblings or living with none.
- Five-minute school trips to over an hour.
- Loving parent to abusive partner.
- Strict to easy-going household ... and the list goes on.

This made it difficult for me to establish a firm foundation with good disciplines and behaviours. The trouble is, I knew that when I went to the other parents' household (whichever way it was), there were certain things I could get away with, so I was given the power to pick and choose. As a child, it's hard to make wise decisions in this situation. One of the most difficult aspects of having my parents separate was living in two very different and extreme households.

Makayla

I don't think I know what was the most difficult, but one definite challenge was those special occasions: birthdays, Christmas and all the others were pretty much split in two. Everything was rushed to get it all done in the available time. And I guess you miss out on those 'happy family' moments with both parents being there. Everything is literally split. Another difficult aspect is missing out on seeing your two biggest role models show you how to love romantically and model what a healthy relationship looks like.

Brooke

What do I believe I missed out on because of my parents' divorce? Everyone's circumstances differ, however I think the loss of being 'a family' is part of all divorces. This has more impact on a child, no matter how old they are, than I think most people seem to realise. As my parents divorced when I was three years old, I never experienced the true meaning of family. I never saw my parents happy together, showing me what it truly meant to love another person.

In some ways I am grateful that my parents divorced when I was young, as I don't know anything different. Although I lived three years with my parents together, I have limited to no recollection of what that felt like. Now for 17 years of my life, my reality has been divorced parents. That doesn't mean I prefer it this way, but that it is all I have ever known. I believe this can be an advantage for younger children as I feel my transition into the 'divorced lifestyle' was much smoother than for my older siblings who were more aware of what was going on and had acquired a larger bank of family memories to reminisce on.

This is not to say however that the younger children are when divorce occurs, the less impact it will have on them. As I have grown up, the effect of my parents' divorce on me personally has become increasingly evident. Living week-to-week alternating between my parents' households was not only physically tiring, it was emotionally draining.

My siblings experienced more years of our parents being together and they gained a stronger sense of 'family' than I did. Despite not understanding what was going on at the time, like any young child I wanted both my parents around, which I unfortunately missed out on. Of course, there are a few perks like receiving double the number of presents at Christmas and birthdays, but I would happily lose all of that if it meant being able to come home every day from school and see both my parents in the one house and call that 'home'.

I am now 21 and think the disadvantages and struggles of having divorced parents change as dynamics shift and you discover more about yourself and the life you wish to live. Despite how long my parents have been divorced, I still want to be able to enjoy special moments with both parents in the same room without any awkwardness, however sometimes that just isn't possible. That is the hard reality of divorce.

2. What do you see as the pros and cons of living in the shared custody of both parents? Would you have preferred to live with just one parent?

Leo

I think there are many pros and cons of living in shared custody.

Cons: from my experience, as I said earlier, one of the greatest disadvantages of living in shared custody is living in different environments when alternating between parents. The dissimilarity can be vast. My personal experience was towards the extreme end. Ponder this, if we developed an equation that determines the harmful effect different living environments may have on a child, I think one of the greatest variables in that equation is the differences in parental beliefs and values. The bigger this gap is, the more it affects our ability as children to find clear direction in life and discover who we are.

Pros: I'm glad that I was able to live with both my parents. This gave me the opportunity to share life equally with them (fifty-fifty) and make good memories of time spent with each parent. If both households offer a healthy living environment, I think shared custody will offer the best opportunity to develop healthy relationships with both parents. It also means the children get the best each parent has to offer.

Despite the fact that living with both parents equally can be seen as a good thing, this doesn't mean that it was best for me. The entire ten years

I lived fifty-fifty with my parents was particularly hard with one parent. From eight to eighteen years I experienced much trauma and emotional hurt that I now wish I had never gone through. I'm a firm believer that God works all things for the good of those who love Him, however if I could go back and choose between the two, I would choose to live with one parent.

Makayla

Looking back, it was definitely hard having shared custody, but I think it's extremely important to do it! I think a lot of it comes down to age. Every kid wants to see their mum and dad. I remember crying on the Sunday changeover when I was young because I missed mum or dad. Packing your bags to change houses, making sure you had everything, then saying goodbye sucked! But looking back, at least I got to see my dad as much as I saw my mum. I think other aspects like having two different households and two different levels of rules made it hard, but I'm still glad that we had shared custody. My views come from having two parents who were 100% fit to look after us kids.

If I hadn't had a choice and I was told I'd be living with one parent 24/7 and seeing the other on occasional weekends – or whatever the arrangement was – I think at the age I am today (in my 20's) I would see two possible outcomes. First, I would have a worse relationship with one, if not both of my parents because I was stopped from having a strong relationship with the one I didn't live with and would possibly have a grudge against the parent I did live with. Or perhaps I would have an amazing relationship with the parent I lived with 24/7, but a massive grudge against the parent I didn't live with because, in my mind, they didn't want me. Perhaps I believe this because I was six at the time of the divorce. If I had been 16 or older, I would probably have different views because I would have been more independent.

There are pros and cons in all situations. In this situation I think the cons are often the 'in the moment' problems, but the pros are emotional and mental, and become obvious later in life.

Brooke

There are definitely pros and cons in living in shared custody. I was fortunate that it was safe to live with both my parents after the divorce. This is not the case for many families. As I look back to alternating between homes week-to-week, it definitely wasn't easy. Having to pack a bag to bring to our other 'home', making sure you remembered everything from school clothes and books to sports uniforms was definitely draining. After a while it took its toll. We could never get into a routine as our environment was constantly changing.

In 2013, after nearly ten years of alternating between homes week-by-week, I decided to live with Dad full-time. This was not an easy decision. It created a wedge between me and Mum and my siblings. I was simply over feeling as if I had no stability in my life. This decision was my way of taking some control. This definitely came with disadvantages, as I rarely saw my Mum and only saw my siblings at school. This made me feel as though they weren't my siblings anymore, but just people in my life who I used to know.

When my parents divorced, the sense of 'family' was broken. Therefore, I believe the most important thing to ensure stayed intact was the bond between us siblings. For me, it felt as though it was us three against the world. My siblings were my anchors throughout the transition into 'divorced lifestyle' and are to this day. Although our environment was ever-changing, we always had each other. Despite being only three years old, I knew something wasn't right and that something had changed. If we kids hadn't had each other, I don't think we would have been able to adjust as well as we did. Additionally, we wouldn't be as close as we are today as, for most of our lives, our only sense of stability has been the bond between us.

Despite these challenges, if I had a choice to live in shared custody or with only one parent, I would still choose shared custody as packing that bag every Sunday meant that I got to see my other parent for a week. Not seeing your parents together is hard, but not being able to see one of your parents at all during childhood is even harder. During childhood you are much more dependent and in need of your parents' love and support. If there is one thing I have learnt and come to appreciate since my parents' divorce, it is that both a dad and a mum bring so much to a family. What is brought by each is entirely different, but of equal value. No matter what age they are, children need both parents in their life. I am so grateful I had the opportunity to experience that, despite not being a 'family' anymore.

3. What do you wish your parents had done differently after the divorce?

Leo

Divorce opens a door for new people to come into our lives; people who can be almost as important as our birth parents. I'm talking about new partners. If and when our parents find a new partner, they are repeating the most significant decision of their lives. I want to stress the importance and implications of this decision. If both parents remarry, the child gains two additional parental figures. Great, now we have four parents – more than anyone else could dream of having. This can be a great thing, however the child is left to witness the baggage that comes along, and some sadly find themselves responsible to carry the load. Two more people, both with a new set of strengths and gifts, but also with a fresh set of flaws and personal struggles. If not made wisely, the decision to remarry can have detrimental effects on a child. Parents bringing someone new into their life are also deciding who their children will spend their life with. I wish all the partners my parents brought into my life were there to love and support. Their decisions greatly affected me. For a long time, I wanted three role models rather than four. I beseech parents to seriously consider who they want to spend their life with again.

Makayla

To be completely honest, I don't know. When I really think about this question, there isn't a list of things I wish were done differently. I'm happy with the person I've become. One thing comes to mind and I can't even stress how important this is. Never disparage the other parent to your kids. It's hard enough to accept that your family is broken, it's quite another thing to bad mouth their own parent to a child.

Brooke

If it's possible to 'do divorce well' I think my parents did a pretty good job. However, if I could go back and change one thing, it would be for my parents not to act like the victim and try to make us 'side with them' in the divorce. In many circumstances this may have not always have been their intention, but it simply happened subconsciously.

Divorce happens for a range of reasons – reasons that are different for every family. However, I don't believe a three-year-old – or even a ten-year-old – needs to know the overarching reason for their parents' divorce. Finding out key information when I was in late primary school regarding one of my parents' choices which ultimately led to their divorce, drastically changed the way in which I viewed and interacted with both my parents. When I discovered those pieces of the puzzle, I naturally drew closer to one parent and in contrast,distanced myself from the other. As this new information did not come directly from the parent whose choice they were but instead from other individuals, their opportunity to tell me their side of the story was taken away. It wasn't until many years later they felt it was time to explain what had happened. By then it was too late. So much anger and hurt had been stored up inside me during those years. When the time came for them to explain their side of the story, no matter what they said, I felt as though I couldn't block out those feelings. It was impossible to have an open mind and genuinely hear what they had to say. I have never had a strong, comforting, nurturing relationship with this parent for numerous reasons, however indirectly finding out key information about them regarding the divorce at such a young age, undoubtedly had a negative impact on our relationship which remains until this day.

Additionally, there were many times when my parents spoke negatively about the other parent in front of us. Dad might be hurt by Mum, Mum might be angry at Dad, however that's between them. I believe children should not be involved as this helps to create a divide within the family. There is hurt and pain in all cases of divorce, however under no circumstances should children be brought into that. The kids should not be made to feel that they need to choose a side or be involved in parental disputes. This only leads to more conflict and potential resentment. Divorce is not the fault of the children and therefore I believe it is best to leave them out of all the technicalities. Just allow them to grow up and learn about themselves. They will reach an age where they begin asking questions and are then old enough to understand the responses eventually given.

Discussion Starters

- Seemingly harmless comments can have lasting consequences.
- It is very important to maintain sibling relationships as they are the remaining semblance of family.
- Children's love for parents is equal and gracious.
- Children can recover well from a broken family.
- Listen to your children.

ELEVEN

Single Again And Loving It

Loving it?! Loving it?! What do you mean I should be loving it? This is not where I'm supposed to be. I'm supposed to still be married to the woman I love, providing for and taking care of our children – building the family God always planned for us to have. I'm supposed to be helping others do the same, being a strong leader in the church and serving the Lord day after day!

That was my inward response when someone would come to me during my darkest times, saying, 'It's awesome. You're single again!'

Did they mean that somehow this divorce was a blessing and I should be glad to have freedom again? I understand that they were just trying to make me feel better by being caring and considerate. They were just trying to help. But please note, it doesn't help. Please keep those sorts of comments to yourself. They give such a sad picture of marriage. Interestingly, those sorts of comments usually came from married guys. I wondered what sort of marriage they were in.

The simple truth is that after a divorce you are 'single again', but for me at the age of 34 that was a weird place to be. I love the Lord more than anything or anyone else, and I try very hard to love God's people, His church, of which I am a part, but going through a divorce gave me a very big wake-up call. God's people sometimes treat the divorced as the modern day 'lepers' of the church.

Before you react with anger or outrage, consider this. One of the first things I did as our marriage started falling apart was to distance myself from my local church and from many Christian friends. Why? As a divorced man, I found the church environment an unsafe place. I wonder if this is a bloke thing. My current wife Lorraine had a very different experience. The church community was probably her main support network.

I remember saying to a close Christian friend – in his early fifties and never married, 'The church community doesn't know how to communicate with me now that I am divorced'.

His blunt and matter of fact response was, 'Welcome to my world!'

He wasn't divorced of course, but the fact that he was still single and in his early 50's didn't fit the church's healthy person stereotype. We as God's church need to stop stereotyping people and accept them as they are – as Jesus does. In fact, it's more than that. Not only accept them, but love them, modeling Jesus' love and acceptance.

Another lesson I learnt was that ...

Divorce can be the catalyst for God to take you somewhere He wants you to go.

Am I saying that God wanted me to get divorced? Not at all. But God knew I was going to get divorced and He also knew what was next – in my life, Jenny's life and your life. God has a plan for our lives. Yet, it still felt as if I had been cast into exile when my marriage broke down. I felt sent to the land of loneliness. Yet, just as God promised His people when they were sent into exile, He was saying to me, 'I know the plans I have for you, declares the Lord, plans for welfare and not for evil, to give you a future and a hope' (Jeremiah 29:11).

The fact that I and so many in our society have been through a divorce is an indictment on our society, our sinful nature and our human ability to stuff things up. God's plan and purpose for us is very different. One of the great privileges God gives every person – followers of Jesus included – is the right to genuinely make our own choices. This right sometimes has terrible and lifelong consequences, but God allows that. At times I can picture Jesus with his head in His hands, shaking it from side to side, saying, 'Father, why do I have to tolerate these people?'

Single Again And Loving It

Yet God's people still belong to Jesus. We are still part of His Kingdom. We call His acceptance of us 'grace'. This was something I never understood before my divorce. I was one of those people who treated divorcees in the congregation as if they were lepers.

In my efforts to 'find myself again', I started church hopping. I lost count of how many churches I visited during a 12-month period – it was a lot. I was on a journey of discovery.

One Sunday I had a life-changing experience. I visited a church someone had recommended. It met in an old factory building, quite close to where I was living. My friend didn't turn up, so I knew no-one. This was rather awkward, yet also freeing. I sat quietly at the back of the church. It was a very small congregation, so it was quite hard to be invisible, even though I tried. The worship music started. They had a modest and very amateur setup – not like the stage show performances many churches have. I stayed seated during the worship because it was a church where people could worship as they wished – and I 'wished' to stay seated.

I sat there, watching the pastor sing – he couldn't sing very well. I can't explain what happened next. You might think I'm crazy, but 'in the Spirit' I 'saw' Jesus up on the stage dancing. I didn't see Jesus physically up on the stage, I just knew He was there. His dancing was slow, involving all his limbs – as if He was simply enjoying himself. Fifteen years later I can still vividly remember the scene. Perhaps it was a vision given by the Holy Spirit – I don't know. I was filled with peace as He danced.

The room had seating in the middle with the aisles along the sides. As the music continued, Jesus stopped dancing, walked across the stage, down the left aisle, across the back and stood right behind me. I was sitting with my arms crossed in a stubborn 'leave me alone' frame of mind.

Jesus gestured for me to stand up and join in the worship. I was still looking straight ahead. I didn't turn around to look at Him, but I knew He was behind me and I knew what He wanted me to do. I refused to get up. Jesus continued walking along the back, up the right aisle, back onto the stage and continued dancing with an expression of joy on his face. I saw nothing physically. You could call it a vision. Remembering and writing this brings tears. I remember nothing else about that service except for the absolute humility of the setting and those present. What was Jesus showing me?

I believe He was showing me that my divorce could be a major catalyst in a renewed journey to discover who Jesus is. Through this experience, Jesus made Himself and His love for me very, very personal.

> *Regardless of the circumstances of my life I can still worship Jesus and bathe in His unconditional love.*

The difficulty people in the church often have in supporting divorced people is sad. My experience was that the church was able to show grace and acceptance to non-believers, or pre-believers who were divorced. Perhaps they thought their divorce was not surprising as they didn't know Jesus. But I was asked questions like, 'What happened to your marriage? What did you do wrong? I hope your experience of support from God's people during a separation or divorce is more positive than mine.

Eventually I settled back into a church community and gradually realised that many other members of the congregation were divorced. Initially it was awkward. People saw me attending church with three children, with a wife nowhere to be seen. I would see the puzzled looks on their faces. They looked at me, they looked at the children, then they looked for the other parent – then they looked back at me. I would wait for the question and prepare myself to answer – an answer driven by my mood at the time. Usually nothing was said and there was an awkward silence until weather became the focal conversation topic.

So, you are on your own now, like it or not. It is a strange situation. Everything you have known has changed. Even if your marriage broke down after a short time, your mindset and headspace spoke the married language. Now you're in the transition period from once married to single.

You may find that friendships start to change as you learn which friends can cope with your new situation. You may remember earlier in my story that at one point God told me who I was not to associate with. You too may find you have to break ties with certain people who are not part of your recovery network, even if the break is only for a time. You may also find that certain people will stop wanting to be with you. They all have their reasons. Some simply don't know how to communicate with you. Some feel like they need to take sides. Sometimes old relationships may re-surface in new and improved ways. I reconnected with people I hadn't seen or spent time with in many years.

Jenny had a married sister. I never had much to do with her husband, Johnson, simply because we were very different people. Sadly, their marriage also broke down. I had no communication with either of them for six months, then Johnson and I re-connected and our relationship went to a whole new level. The focus of conversation was our marriage breakdowns. Previously we had nothing in common, but we become best mates and were best man at each other's second marriage. This new relationship was a beautiful gift from God. Our favourite friendship Bible verse was Proverbs 27:17 – 'iron sharpens iron, and one man sharpens another'. I believe God puts the right people in the right place at the right time. Eighteen years later, we still connect on a regular basis and have continued with the 'sharpening'. We live more than 2000 kms apart so it is difficult to see one another face to face but, when we do connect we have a very special time.

Even though your new-found singleness may come with the loss of some – perhaps many – friendships, it will strengthen other relationships and perhaps lead to many new ones. These changes may be part of your grief recovery process.

The loss of friendships is likely to add an additional sense of loss to a marriage breakdown.

Give yourself time to process this grief – to reflect on past friendships – what they meant to you. The level of grief in relation to those lost friendships will reveal how dependent you were on those friends. God certainly showed me that my dependency was on a number of other things and people, rather than on Him.

You may be contacted by past friends in various ways for a variety of reasons. It takes time to assess the motivation behind a lot of that communication. Your support network can really help you unpack comments from past friends.

One of the things I struggled with greatly after my divorce was the complete absence of communication from Jenny's extended family. I had deep relationships with many of them and those relationships came to a screeching halt. It grieved me deeply and, to be honest, greatly disappointed me. Once I realised why they felt it was necessary to cut off communication, I was able to accept it. I did not agree, but I accepted it and moved on with my recovery.

Early on it is important to be with people who are safe and positive, but there was a period where I simply didn't want to be with anyone. This was OK for a time, but there comes a time when you need to pick yourself up, drag yourself out of bed, open your front door and interact with others again. You will know when the right time comes. If your isolation starts dragging on too long, allow your trusted friends to give you some tough love.

One of the things I found very difficult was being a single parent! I take my hat off to all you mums and dads who do parenting alone. Parenting is hard enough as a married couple, but doing it alone is tough! I was not exactly 'domesticated', so I quickly had to learn how to do the washing, brush my girls' hair, cook meals ... If you ask my kids, they will say I never did get the hang of cooking. The microwave and precooked meals were my best friends. My motto was just 'add water'. I had to laugh one day when my kids and I were around the dinner table reminiscing about those days. My eldest daughter Makayla confessed to loathing a particular meal. She would put the meat-filled pasta I dished up down in her socks. How did I not notice that at the time? I only found out ten years later. The other kids knew. Funny. In my defence, I made a pretty mean spaghetti bolognaise. I hated cooking and still do. Just as well they got fed well at their mum's house.

Guys, it's OK that we are not chefs! It's OK to let other people assist with the preparation of meals as you settle into single parenthood.

My girls gave me a lot of grace. I remember having to ask a school mum over to my place early one morning when school photos were being taken later that day. I asked her to do my girls' hair so they didn't look as if they had just climbed out of bed. We certainly showed up at church with the kids looking as if they were just out of bed. There was no need to ask if I was a single dad in those days! I would often show up at work meetings with a stretchy around my wrist because we had just had a hair episode. One thing I learnt very quickly was that it was OK, in fact it was often essential, to ask for help. A bit of humbling never went astray for me. Make sure you read the insights from my kids in Chapter 10 if you haven't done so already. My children coped well in a very sad and difficult situation – praise God!

After a while I did enjoy 'being single again'. I learned so much about myself, about relationships, about my children, about life and about how to do things better next time. I learned a lot from my past mistakes and from the mistakes of others. Most importantly I was able to establish a real relationship with Jesus which I had never previously understood was possible.

Discussion Starters

- Give people time to understand and accept your new circumstances.
- There are more people in your situation than you realise.
- Old friendships will be lost and new ones established.
- Don't try to be a super dad or a super mum.
- Seek to thrive in the relationship with your children.
- Be intentional about having fun.
- Let yourself laugh, even over the silly stuff.

TWELVE

New Relationship

I can honestly say the thought of a new relationship didn't enter my mind until at least six months after the separation – and that thought made me feel ill. It had taken a good six months for the knot in my stomach to start to subside. Given all the issues I was working through as a result of the divorce, I had enough to think about without dealing with a new relationship. Yet God has designed us for relationship and companionship.

I remember a friend I deeply respect saying to me, 'Don't get remarried too soon.' Well that is what I heard, but I think he actually said 'Don't get remarried!'

Easy for him to say. Being a strong believer in the truth of God's Word I had to investigate what it meant for a man of God to remarry. I am not going to go into the theology of marriage and remarriage – I will leave that for you to work through – but it was certainly something I had to process. It was at least 12 months before I was ready to entertain the idea that remarriage may be for me. Given the difficult process of recovering from a broken marriage, the thought of exploring the issue of remarriage was emotionally exhausting. There were so many questions:

- Does God want me to remarry?
- Does God allow me to remarry?
- What will my kids think about me getting remarried?
- If my first marriage didn't work, what are the chances of a second marriage working?

- What sort of baggage would another woman bring into our marriage?
- Where am I going to find the type of woman I deserve (selfish, but true)
- What will people think of me if I remarry?
- Is it selfish of me to remarry?
- Will I lose my kids if I remarry?

These were my questions as a bloke. I suspect the questions from a woman's perspective might look something like this:

- Who is going to want to marry me now?
- How can another guy love and care for my children?
- What if he does the same thing my first husband did?
- What will people, especially my friends think of me?
- What if my kids don't like him? (requires a lot of processing this one.)

Remember how we talked about truth and lies in previous chapters? This was certainly one of those occasions where I was having to sort out the truth from the lies. You may be thinking, *Great I get to hear the answer to some of my questions.* Sorry, you will need to work out your own answers, with the help of your trusted network of wise friends. But be careful with other people's advice. There will be no shortage of 'friends' ready to give you their opinion and the reasons for that opinion. I became quite experienced in discerning the motivation behind people's advice. I am the type of guy who generally gets as much advice as I can. Then I take what I like and throw away the rest. The real challenge comes when I don't like the advice, but know that it is true and correct.

As you make your own list of questions, I suggest you write them down for future reference. It is also wise to identify which questions are important to answer and which are not.

I am very glad that I did not need another relationship. I have seen both men and women desperate to find another partner. This can be unhealthy.

Many of us want relationship and companionship, but if it becomes a need, especially a desperate one, there can be serious problems.

If you have given yourself the time to evaluate and recover from your failed marriage, you are less likely to fall into another unhealthy relationship. I have met a number of people, men in particular, who are in a third or even a fourth marriage. I can only imagine the trail of destruction those marriages represent. But remember ...

The more self-evaluation we do, the less likely we are to have another broken relationship.

Self-evaluation helps you to understand yourself and to take great care when choosing another partner.

I was single again, but I was not looking for marriage. I chose to leave that in God's hands. In addition, I was so busy looking after three children, running my own business, maintaining a house and simply trying to survive. After a time, I started socialising again and meeting new people. A group of us at the church I was attending established a singles group for 'older' people – a group full of divorced men and women. It was an eye opener into the destructive world of divorce.

There were so many hurting mums and broken dads, all finding life extremely tough. I realised that I had to have my 'damaged person' radar on. If you thought finding a life partner was hard as a young person, try looking for a life partner as a man or woman in your 30s among many other damaged men and women. One thing was certain – there was never any shortage of topics to discuss.

I suggest that you make a list of your desires and needs in a future partner – a wish list if you like. Include non-negotiables and negotiables and what I like to classify as 'run!' After meeting a couple of women, I started to get a picture of what I did and didn't want in a life partner.

I met some great people and for many of us past failures were healed during these meetings. The meetings weren't necessarily structured, but the casual atmosphere was all the more effective. It became obvious that there were many lonely men and women looking for companionship. It also became obvious which of them had done a lot of soul searching and took recovery seriously, and who was just looking for the next relationship. Let me make some rather frank observations.

Dating at a more mature age is very different from dating in your late teens. We may carry more baggage into our next relationship. This makes the following dating principles very important. Many of these are true for dating at any age, but there is a lot more to consider when you are older. Remember you are looking for the person you want to spend the rest of your life with. It is important to:

- Spend a significant amount of time getting to know the person.
- Involve yourself in their network of friends. This will help you get to know them.
- Involve them with your network of friends and observe how they interact.
- Observe how they interact with other people.
- Observe how other people interact with them.
- If you are a person of faith, observe their faith commitment.
- When it is safe, be prepared to be open and honest with them about every issue relating to your previous broken marriage – and I mean everything!
- Be prepared to answer any questions they may have.

- Gain an understanding of everything involved in the breakdown of their previous relationship
- Understand their attitude to money and possessions.
- Know if they want to enter into a prenuptial agreement.
- If they have children, observe the way they interact with their children and how their children interact with them.
- Observe how they interact with your children and how your children interact with them.
- Gain a strong understanding of their personality type (*Personality Plus* by Florence Littaeur is a wonderful reference book).
- Gain a strong understanding of their love language (*The Five Love Languages* by Gary Chapman is a must read).
- Be prepared to walk away from the relationship at any time before marriage no matter how much you have invested in the relationship.

There are some behaviours that should ring alarm bells for you. Guys, there's a rather obvious one from a man's perspective. If you are thinking more with your penis than with your head and heart, then you may be very well be heading for another period of pain. Ladies, if the man you are dating thinks more of his penis than of you, beware!

Men, beware of women who come onto you very strongly, especially if they have children. I saw a number of situations where women were looking for a father for their children, rather than for a husband to spend the rest of their lives with.

These are just general observations. The reality is there is never any guarantee of a successful relationship or marriage. We are fallen people living in a fallen world. Guys, can I also say that if you are waiting for what I like to call the female version of Jesus, then you will remain single for the rest of your life. With all the safeguards in place,

It is not about looking for perfection, rather, working our way through imperfection.

From the perspective of a Jesus follower, it is easy to advise you to wait until Jesus brings the right woman or man along for you, *yer yer, we all get that*, but we have some work to do along the way to find her or him.

I have already mentioned a number of times that I have remarried. Lorraine and I married at the end of May 2009, approximately five years after the breakdown of my first marriage. How did I meet Lorraine? I now realise that Jesus brought her to me. I was working from a rented home, after selling my first marital home as part of the divorce settlement. I had converted the lounge into a makeshift office, had a week on week off shared custody agreement for our three children and was in the middle of custody discussions with Jenny.

I received a phone call from a woman who was wanting to get back into the workforce. Lorraine had previously worked as a manual structural draftsperson, but had not worked in the construction industry for over ten years and needed to learn computer drafting. She asked if I could assist her in any way. I was very busy at the time and simply said that she could come and teach herself on the spare office computer. Lorraine came in one day a week. I handed her the manual and pretty much left her to it. After about four months, she was becoming quite proficient and I offered her some work. It was a win win for both of us.

I was in the middle of some very difficult divorce challenges and Lorraine was a great listening ear. I would often vent my frustrations in the office. I was certainly not looking for a relationship at this time, but her friendship was much appreciated. After about six months I realised that Lorraine was a woman of integrity and my attraction to her grew. I was observing her as a woman, a mother and a follower of Jesus. Unbeknownst to me, Lorraine was also observing me. We proved to be compatible in many ways and she met most of my criteria for a life partner.

I put Lorraine through the wringer. I had so many questions, concerns and fears as a result of my divorce. She was so much more gracious and fearless than I was. There is a lot at stake when it comes to a second marriage, especially when I had three young children and Lorraine had four. We were certainly called the Brady bunch, minus the maid – who would have been very helpful!

How do I know God brought her to me? With seven children between us, we needed a big house. I didn't have a big house. I had just bought a single storey, four-bedroom house just around the corner from the house I was renting. I said to God, 'If You want me to marry Lorraine, I need $90,000 to extend this house – and quickly would be nice.'

Within three months I had the $90,000, but it didn't just turn up on our doorstep. Only God knew about my request. I didn't even tell Lorraine. At that time Australia was coming out of a recession and the Australian government introduced an economic stimulus package called the 'Building Education Revolution'. Schools were given millions of dollars for building projects that had to be done in a very short time. I had three school clients at that time and my workload exploded. We worked very hard and, within three months had the $90,000. God has His ways.

We knew that the fallout from another broken marriage would be very severe – on seven children and the extended family. We spent at least two years working through all the implications and dynamics of what it meant for us to be married – and there were many! We have now been married for 11 years. As we look back we are amazed by the goodness of God – and by how hard it has been! Yet, despite all the tough situations, I have learnt how fantastic a marriage could be. We have a long way to go but the journey has been, and continues to be, an awesome one.

I mentioned very early on in this book that divorce is not the end of your story and that there is certainly life after divorce, whether you end up remarried or not. I believe God wanted me to write this book to help people going through a divorce not only to recover from divorce, but thrive through the recovery.

There is life after divorce – not just life, but a fulfilling, joyful life, filled with laughter and emotional freedom.

You can have a life where you can love someone again and have an amazing marriage – as God designed and intended marriage to be. Your children can also thrive, becoming young adults of responsibility and purpose, establishing their own identity and living joyous fulfilling lives.

I can honestly declare these things to be true because I have lived that story and continue to do so. You can endure through the hard work of recovery, picking yourself back up after repeated mistakes and failures. You can learn what it means to trust again, love again and laugh until your stomach hurts. You can be a husband and father – a wife and mother – of far greater capacity than you were or could be before.

I have not done this journey on my own. I have journeyed with many people along the way, some for a short time, others for a longer time, but one, in particular has journeyed with me through the whole time and I know He will journey with me for the rest of my story – Jesus. I don't know how I could have recovered without Him, or indeed if I would have. So, if you want the best recovery possible, let Jesus help you. How? Just ask Him – then stop and listen.

Discussion Starters

- Don't rush into another relationship.
- Spend time evaluating past mistakes and misunderstandings.
- Write a list of desires for a future relationship.
- Be prepared to walk away before marriage regardless of how much you have invested in the relationship.
- Seek the counsel of trusted friends.
- Allow God to be part of your relationship.
- Remember, marriage is God's wonderful design for people.

www.ingramcontent.com/pod-product-compliance
Lightning Source LLC
Chambersburg PA
CBHW070308010526
44107CB00056B/2533